Praise for Master Zhongxian Wu's
Seeking the Spirit of The Book of Change

"You hold in your hands one of the finest interpretations of the *I Ching* on the planet. Master Wu artfully presents a clear and insightful interpretation of ageless wisdom for seekers of consciousness in these troubled times. I highly suggest bringing a cup of hot water to boil, infusing it with your favorite blend of tea, and curling up with this book."

—*Brian Luke Seaward, Ph.D., author of*
Stand Like Mountain, Flow Like Water

"At first glance, this remarkable book may appear to be a straightforward guide to the symbolism and interpretation of the Eight Trigrams (Bagua) of the Chinese classic known as the *Book of Change*. In outline, it follows the pattern as an eight-day course, illustrated with case histories along the way. With its carefully ordered structure, attention to detail, and diligence in referring to sources, it has all the hallmarks of a book written by a master of the subject. But this is no mere scholarly tome; its author Master Wu addresses the reader directly, offering tea, then describing the physical and mental exercises which need to be done before approaching the next section, and often inviting his personal guest, the reader, to join him for a meal or a walk through the woods at the close of a course of study. This is a fascinating and engrossing way to tackle one of the most enigmatic texts of world literature."

—*Derek Walters, Founder of The School of Feng Shui and author*

"Wu Zhongxian combines a deep knowledge of ancient Chinese traditions, a keen awareness of the needs of his Western audience, and a unique ability to communicate between the two. Such a combination is rare in a world of specialists and dilettantes, and his latest effort couldn't come at a more opportune time. There is always room for one more in his Celestial Tea House. I hope to see you there."

—*Bill Porter (Red Pine), author of* Road to Heaven

"Master Wu's book is really an invitation to spend a week with a practicing Taoist, and as such it is a unique and refreshing addition to the literature of the *Yijing*. He presents a traditional method of divination that relies on a balance of philosophy and intuition, on numerology, and on wordless awareness. Master Wu invites us into his tea room, introduces us to the culture of tea and the practice of Qigong. His goal is admirable. Let's not be mere students of the *Yijing* but find that state of mind and unity with the Tao from which the *Yijing* was first produced."

—*Kenneth Cohen, author of* The Way of
Qigong and Taoism: Essential Teachings

"In past decades, countless new attempts have been made to delve into the mystery and wisdom of the *I Ching*, from the most astute to the inane variations. It is a special treat to read this new perspective of Master Wu's entry into this ancient classic through the Shamanic Prediction Systems. Master Wu has made this often indecipherable exotic way accessible; and it is especially delightful that he is inviting the reader into this process by sharing a cup of good tea while along the way, introducing the Tao of Tea. I highly recommend this book as another worthy supplement to all lifelong students of the *I Ching*."

—*Chungliang Al Huang, Founder of the Living Tao Foundation,
Director of the International Lan Ting Institute, and author of*
Embrace Tiger, Return To Mountain

Seeking the Spirit of The Book of Change

8 Days to Mastering a Shamanic Yijing (I Ching) Prediction System

MASTER ZHONGXIAN WU

FOREWORD BY DANIEL REID

SINGING DRAGON
London and Philadelphia

First published in 2009
by Singing Dragon
an imprint of Jessica Kingsley Publishers
116 Pentonville Road
London N1 9JB, UK
and
400 Market Street, Suite 400
Philadelphia, PA 19106, USA

www.singing-dragon.com

Copyright © Master Zhongxian Wu 2009
Foreword copyright © Daniel Reid 2009

Library of Congress Cataloging in Publication Data
A CIP catalog record for this book is available from the Library of Congress

British Library Cataloguing in Publication Data
A CIP catalogue record for this book is available from the British Library

ISBN 978 1 84819 020 7

Printed and bound in the United States by
Thomson-Shore, 7300 Joy Road, Dexter, MI 48130

When you play divination, do no thinking, do no
action, be silent, be still, and resonate your heart with the
universe to clearly perceive the result of everything.

Xici 繫辭 *(Appended Statements)* of *Yijing*

Dedicated to the Hidden Immortal Lineage and
Master Yang Rongji/Yongji 楊榮籍/永積

Contents

FOREWORD: ONE TASTE, BY DANIEL REID 13

ACKNOWLEDGMENTS.. 17

Introduction: *Yijing* Prediction and Wu 巫 (Shamanism): *Yuanqi* 緣起 19

About the Title of *Yijing*...................................... 20

Wu 巫: Chinese Shamanism 23

Wu 巫 and Chinese Culture 25

The Secret of *Yijing*.. 28

The Spirit of *Yijing* 30

1. Dao 道: The Way of Yi 易 and Tea.................................. 37

The Celestial Tea House 38

Tea Ceremony 40

The Secret of the Universe 43

Tea and the Dao 道 45

Gua 卦 (Trigram or Hexagram) 47

Taiji Qigong Qian 乾 (Heaven) 50

2. Yi 易: The Change and Myths 55

A Story of Creation and Gua 卦 (Trigram) 56

Tea and Yi 易 (Divination) 60

Fuxi 伏羲: The First Chinese Shaman King...................... 64

Bagua 八卦: The Eight Trigrams Arrangements 67

Taiji Qigong Dui 兌 (Lake)..................................... 70

3. Shu 數: Numerology 75
Shudao 數道: The Way of the Numbers 75
Hetu 河圖 and Luoshu 洛書: The Patterns of the Universe 78
Tiandi Shengcheng Shu 天地生成數: Heaven and Earth Creating and
Completing Numbers 86
The Relationships among Numerology, Yin-Yang, and Five Elements 88
Xiantian Bagua Shu 先天八卦數: Prenatal Eight Trigrams Numbers 89
Taiji Qigong Li 離 (Fire) 93

4. Xiang 象: Symbolism 99
Xiang 象: Symbolism 100
Guaxiang 卦象: The Symbolic Meaning of the Bagua 八卦 103
Taiji Qigong Zhen 震 (Thunder) 118

5. Zhan 占: The Divination 123
Qi Gua 起卦: Make a Trigram with a Number 124
Jie Gua 解卦: Decode the Trigram 126
Eight Trigrams and Five Elements 131
Taiji Qigong Xun 巽 (Wind) 140

6. Li 例: Case Analyses 145
Pork Stew 146
Burning Incense and Heart 147
The Magical Mirror 151
Move, Travel, and Hire 154
The Home of Your Soul 158
Taiji Qigong Kan 坎 (Water) 165

7. Chuan 傳: The Hidden Immortal Lineage 171
A Brief Introduction to the Chinese Immortal Cultivation Lineage 172
The Chanting Ceremony 176
Mayi Daozhe 麻衣道者: The Declarer of the Original *Yijing* 181

Xiyi Xiansheng 希夷先生: The First Promoter of Taiji.................... 183

Yang Yongji 楊永積: A Modern Hermit 186

Taiji Qigong Gen 艮 (Mountain)... 189

8. Yao 要: The Essence of the Prediction.................................. 195

Xing 形: Model.. 196

Wuxing 無形: Predicting without a Model 197

Xinfa 心灋: Heart Method 199

Gantong 感通: Inherent Prediction 202

Taiji Qigong Kun 坤 (Earth).. 206

AFTERWORD: LIFE IS THE TREASURE 211
APPENDIX: A MIRACLE STORY OF INNER CULTIVATION
        BY CHERYL SLY 215
ABOUT THE AUTHOR... 219
GLOSSARY 223
INDEX 229

Foreword

One Taste

Daniel Reid

Life is essentially a verb, not a noun. This is the first and foremost lesson in the *I Ching,* or *Yijing* 易經, which is why it's called *The Book of Change.* Movement, activity, process, change—these are the basic facts of life, the fundamental forces of the universe that make the world go round, and we need to understand how they work in order to live life "on Earth as it is in Heaven." Concrete objects, physical bodies, molecular matter, all composite things change their form from moment to moment, and nothing is immutable, immortal, or immune to this ongoing process. In other words,

One taste

Daniel Reid is an internationally respected author in the field of natural medicine and holistic healing, with particular focus on TCM (Traditional Chinese Medicine), detox, and energy medicine. His book *The Tao of Health, Sex, and Longevity* has been published in eight languages, including Chinese. His latest health title is *The Tao of Detox: the Natural Way to Purify Your Body for Health and Longevity* (Simon & Schuster, UK; Inner Traditions, USA). His latest publication is *My Journey in Mystic China: Old Pu's Travel Diary,* his translation from Chinese into English of the writer John Blofeld's memoirs of his life in China from 1930 to 1948 (Inner Traditions, USA).

He currently lives near Byron Bay with his wife Snow, who is well known in Asian healing circles for her popular "Renew Your Lease on Life" integrated detox and regeneration program. More info on his books, articles, and other work may be found on his website: www.danreid.org

there's not a noun on earth that isn't subject to the verb of constant change. In *Wisdom of the Taoists,* D. Howard Smith states this point as follows:

> Seeing that everything, including themselves, is in
> a state of perpetual transition and change, they
> concluded that nothing observable is permanent.
> Nothing has a selfhood of its own. All is in process,
> never remaining the same for one moment.

The second basic premise of the *I Ching* is that the future is a set of infinite possibilities that may be narrowed down to a few fairly certain probabilities, if you understand the dynamics of change and learn how to detect their directional signals in the present. The *I Ching* offers us a precise view of our present situation, identifies the key currents of change that govern it, and indicates how the situation in question is unfolding, where it's leading us, and what choices we can make now in order to influence the process of change in a favorable direction.

Wu Zhongxian's presentation of the *I Ching* is a worthy and highly original contribution to Western scholarship and English literature on this revered Chinese classic, which ranks as the world's most ancient book. As someone who has often consulted the *I Ching*—always in conjunction with a well-versed master—and read most of its English translations, I am well aware that the *I Ching* does not lightly "reveal Heaven's secrets" (*lu tian-ji* 露天機) to those without the right foundation. It responds only to someone who has attained a sufficient degree of finesse in what the Chinese refer to as *xiu-shen yang-xin* 修神養心, literally to "refine the spirit and cultivate the mind." Only such a person is qualified as a vessel for insight and information from such a sacred source. By "sacred" I don't mean "holy"—this is not a matter of religion—I mean the pure, perfect, infinitely potent source of wisdom and power that abides in stillness and silence beyond the temporal world of form and function, a source which only highly polished minds can reflect. It's clear that Master Wu, who is heir to a long and venerable lineage of Tao 道, or Dao 道, masters in China, has refined his spirit and cultivated his mind to the level of wisdom and awareness required for this work, and it's obvious from his discourse that he knows the *I Ching* like an old friend.

Master Wu deals very well with the basic principle of trinity that runs throughout Taoist philosophy and science. We see the fundamental triune nature of human life on earth manifest in the triplex unities of the "Three Powers" (Heaven, Earth, and Humanity), the "Three Treasures" (Essence, Energy, and Spirit), and of course the three lines of the *Bagua* 八卦, the eight core trigrams that lie at the heart of the *I Ching.* Modern Western science is familiar with the duality of mind and matter, the duplexity of energy and mass, and the polarity of positive and negative forces—all of which traditional Chinese science refers to as the "Great Principle of Yin and Yang"—but it doesn't understand the third factor, the one which brings the other two together and breathes life into the equation. That factor is consciousness. Consciousness is the missing link in modern Western science, but it's always been the central fulcrum in traditional Eastern science. Consciousness is the key that unlocks the gates of mystery and magic and bridges the gap between the formless and the formed.

Consciousness is the motive power behind all creation and change, the conductor of the music to which the polar partners of Yin and Yang, Heaven and Earth, male and female dance through the universe. The science of quantum physics has recently verified the decisive role played by consciousness in the transformations of energy and matter, but the *I Ching* has taught this truth for thousands of years. Its pages provide us with a reliable way to foresee how the intricate interplay between the Three Powers of Heaven, Earth, and Humanity (i.e. energy, matter, and spirit) in a person's life now give rise to particular results later, and how the tides of change which mold the future may be favorably influenced by timely decisions in the present.

In a word that always rings a familiar bell for Western readers, consciousness is a "science," just like biology and chemistry, and the *I Ching* is a textbook that explains how this science works, and how intent, attitude, virtue, integrity, and other mental factors decisively influence the outcome of physical events. The *I Ching* maps the invisible paths of mind that wind behind the veils of the visible world and govern the sovereign state of "mind over matter."

I particularly like the way Wu Zhongxian approaches his discussion of the *I Ching* as a friendly tea talk with his readers. This format resonates especially well with me because during my 16-year residence in Taiwan, most of the teachings I received from my own Taoist mentors came across the tea table, not in workshops or classrooms. Tea itself is one of the most ancient arts of China, deeply steeped in the Tao, and thus the tea table lends itself well as a platform for discourse on the subtle patterns in the tapestry of the *I Ching.* Preparing and drinking tea the Chinese way calms the spirit and clarifies the mind, establishing the perfect setting of serene awareness for discussing and consulting the *I Ching.*

Every Tao master I've ever known has also mastered the Way of Tea (*cha dao* 茶道), and Master Wu is no exception. Throughout his discourse, he reminds us that the taste of tea prepared the Chinese way, in accordance with the Tao of Tea, clearly reflects the energy and spirit of the hand that makes it, just as the lines in a hexagram always mirror the prevailing state of energy (change) and spirit (consciousness) in the life of the person who casts it. Indeed, with practice, the taste of tea may well reveal the truth as clearly as the structure of a hexagram, as suggested by one of my favorite pearls of Chinese tea wisdom:

cha chan yi wei 茶禪一味 "Tea and Zen are one taste"

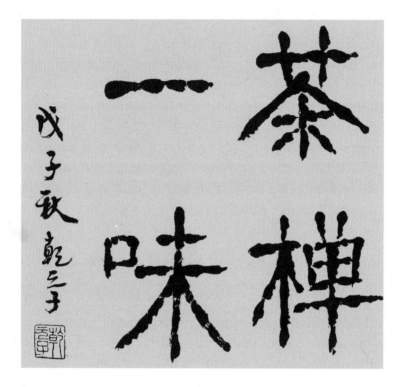

I've read many books about the *I Ching,* in English as well as Chinese, but this is the first one that let me feel its pulse and hear its heart beat. It also taught me some interesting things about tea, which remains my personal favorite of the traditional Chinese arts.

So go prepare yourself a pot of good Chinese tea, do it the traditional Chinese way, and get ready for a personal introduction to the ancient *I Ching,* from someone who is very close to its original source.

Byron Bay, Australia
September 2, 2008
Year of the Earth Rat

Acknowledgments

In Chinese, we have a proverb: San Zu Ding Li 三足鼎立—"With three legs, a Ding (**cauldron**) can be set up." This proverb states when a person wants to do something, in order to be successful, three right conditions must be present to help them achieve the goal. These conditions are (1) Tianshi 天時, Heavenly time; (2) Dili 地利, Earthly benefit; and (3) Renhe 人和, Humanity harmony. At the moment as I'm completing this *Seeking the Spirit of The Book of Change*, I want to express my deepest gratitude to these three conditions:

1. **Tianshi**—Heavenly time, which means the right time for you to do something. Only with wordless words can I express my deep gratitude for the time I have spent with my teachers and parents. They are important sources of my writing. I will continue to hold those moments in my heart for my personal inner cultivation, teaching, and writing. I treasure the time in China I have spent with my brothers and sisters in the Dao to cultivate our inner wisdom together, to take pilgrims to see our teachers and sacred places together, to share our personal experiences on spiritual journeys together. These moments are the inspirations for my writing and my life. I cherish the time I have spent with my students to share the Chinese wisdom traditions; it is a great motivation for my writing and teaching.

2. **Dili**—Earthly benefit, which means the right place for you to achieve your goal. Nature is a great inspiration for my writing. From China to North America, many magical places have inspired my writings and my spiritual cultivation. I appreciate all the places I have been, with those nature spirits, and each breath I take which keeps my spirit uplifted in my daily life. I especially appreciate Salt Spring Island in British Columbia and Cloud Mountain in Castle Rock, Washington, the two main places made available for me to write this book.

3. **Renhe**—Humanity harmony, which means you have a good group of people who can support each other and help you complete your mission. The support from families, friends, publisher, editor, designer, and students is the reason this book became real. I want to acknowledge:

Pamela Causgrove for her professional editing and support on this book and my other writings.

Deirdre Orceyre for her excellent notes on my teachings and support in many ways.

Jessica Kingsley for her suggestions for this book and her Singing Dragon imprint in bringing this book to us.

Daniel Reid for his review of this book, helpful suggestions, and the Foreword.

Kenneth Cohn, Chungliang Al Huang, Bill Porter, Derek Walters, and Brian Luke Seaward for their helpful suggestions and reviews of my book.

Dhammadasa (David Branscomb), Laura Hauer, Adrienne Linder, and Alan Linder for their generous offering of space for my personal retreats and writing.

All my students for their useful *Yijing* prediction case study notes and their support in my teaching.

Nisa Ojalvo and Catalina Maria Gonzalez for taking pictures of my movements.

Finally, I want to thank you for your willingness to read this book. Through pursuing a harmonious life, through seeking the roots of natural healing modalities, through spiritual cultivation, and through your quest for Enlightenment, you keep the ancient wisdom alive.

Live in harmonious Qi!

Zhongxian Wu
Cusheon Lake Cottage, Salt Spring Island, BC
October 21, 2008

Introduction

Yijing Prediction and Wu 巫 (Shamanism) *Yuanqi* 緣起

Seeking the Spirit of The Book of Change: 8 Days to Mastering a Shamanic Yijing (I Ching) Prediction System is a technical prediction book based on the knowledge of Bagua 八卦, the Eight Trigrams of the *Yijing* 易經, that I have shared with students in my Lifelong Training Program. This is the first time I have put on paper this oral prediction knowledge, which has been closely held in the Daoist tradition. However, after having prayed for the support of the universe and my ancestral masters, I have been guided to share this knowledge with those who are ready to receive it.

When you first look at the title of this book, you might be puzzled if you have some previous knowledge about *Yijing*. As you know, the titles of most *Yijing* (*I Ching*) books are translated as *Book of Changes*, using the plural form, Changes. You might wonder why I use the less common singular form, Change. Most people think *Yijing* is a Daoist or Confucian book, so you might have some questions such as: Why do you use "shamanic *Yijing*" in the subtitle? What is shamanism? How is shamanism connected to Daoism and Confucianism? In this introduction, I'll try to answer these questions and provide some information about this book.

ABOUT THE TITLE OF *YIJING*

In the Chinese tradition, the name of an object symbolizes all the information about that object. For instance, a new baby's name is used not only for communication purposes but also contains the baby's personality and life karma. In Chinese, we have a saying, "A person's name comes from the universe." In other words, it doesn't matter who gave you your name—the universe is the original source of your name. The same is true for the names or titles of Chinese classics. The title of a book is the essence and spirit of the book. This book is about *Yijing* prediction systems. Gaining a better understanding of the title of *Yijing* will help us in our study of the *Yijing* and its prediction system.

Yijing is often written as *I Ching* in English. *Yijing* is the Chinese name of *The Book of Change* in pinyin 拼音, the official system of romanization for the Chinese language, and *I Ching* is the name for this book in the Wade-Giles system, which was the most common system of romanization for Chinese before pinyin 拼音 was developed.

Yijing contains two Chinese characters: Yi 易 and Jing 經. We can use the characters Yi and Jing as nouns, verbs, or adjectives. In general, Yi means alternate, shift, change, easy, trade, and communication. Yi is also an abbreviated name of *Yijing*. Jing means thread, pass, straight, vertical, longitude, rule, and classics. Normally, when the title of a Chinese book ends with the character Jing, it means the book is one of the important classics from ancient China. Therefore, *Yijing* is one of the most important ancient Chinese classics about Yi. In the *Yijing* academic field, we have two main opinions about the source of Yi for *Yijing*: (a) from chameleon, because the Chinese name for chameleon is Yi and all chameleon species are able to change their skin color to match their surroundings and play a part in communication; therefore, a chameleon represents the spirit of *Yijing*; (b) from sun and moon, because the Chinese character Yi 易 is made of the upper radical Ri 日 for sun and the bottom radical Yue 月 for moon. Sun represents the Yang 陽 energy and moon represents the Yin 陰 energy; therefore, sun and moon represent the alternating rhythm of the Yin and Yang energies in nature, which perfectly match the philosophy of the *Yijing* book.

In my opinion, the Big Dipper in the sky was the original source of Yi for the *Yijing* title. Two pieces of evidence led me to this conclusion. First, when I examined the ancient Chinese character for Yi, I noticed that the pattern of the character looks like a cup holding water or grain or a dipper pouring out water or grain.[1]

Ancient Chinese named a cup or dipper Dou 斗, the name of the Big Dipper constellation. So, I think that the original meaning of the character Yi is Big Dipper. Second, when I read the *Yijing*, I realized that one of the rhetorical structures for explaining the meaning of each hexagram is to begin with "Tuan Yue 彖曰." Tuan means boar or pig. Archeologist scholars have proved that a symbol for boar or pig stands for the Big Dipper in ancient China.[2] Yue means say or speak. Hence, Tuan Yue means "Boar says" or "Big Dipper indicates."

The Big Dipper is the heart of the celestial world according to Chinese shamanic tradition. Ancient Chinese astronomers called this constellation the "Jade Balance of Fate." It is in charge of the human being's karma and life force. Considered a trigger for natural phenomena occurring in the universe, it is responsible for the unleashing of natural disasters and the releasing of disease. Accordingly, it has the function of governing the universal laws of the four seasons. It is thought to govern the general balance of Yin and Yang in the universe.

Yi (a cup holding water or grain)

Yi (a dipper pouring out water or grain)

A clay vessel decorated with a pig on each side discovered in Zhejiang province, from about 7000 years ago

---

1   *Great Dictionary of Chinese Characters* (Chengdu: Sichuan Chishu Chubanshe, 1996: 696).

2   Feng, Shi. *Archaeoastronomy in China* (Beijing: Zhongguo Shehui Kexue Chubanshe, 2007: 129–167).

The movement of the Dipper patterns the Yin-Yang movement of the Dao, which indicates the change of nature.

In China, we also call this ancient book *Yijing* "*Tian Shu* 天書" (Heavenly Book). People in ancient China trusted that the knowledge was channeled from Heaven/ sky through Wu 巫, the ancient Chinese shaman. Because of this, Confucius said, "I only record the ancient knowledge without adding my own ideas [when I edit the old classics]. I always trust, respect, and love the ancient knowledge."[3] Han dynasty (206 BCE–220 CE) *Sima Qian* 司馬遷, the author of the *Shiji* 史記, the Book of History, referred to this way of thinking as "the Sage's attitude."[4]

When we read the *Yijing* with insight, we can tell that *Yijing* is essentially about the idea and the process of change as the basic dynamic of the universe. In ancient China, Wu, the enlightened beings, applied the Big Dipper as the main tool to learn about the rhythm and dynamic of change in the universe. And Wu have been using the knowledge of "Change" to guide people's lives into a harmonious state. In China, we also call *Yijing* "Wu Shu," which means "Shamans' Book."

Accordingly, I follow John Blofeld's lead and translate *Yijing* (*I Ching*) as "*The Book of Change*" (not "*Changes*"). Blofeld gives a convincing explanation for using the singular form, not the plural, in the first chapter of his *I Ching* translation:

> My choice of the singular form arises from my conviction that the Chinese authors selected the title to reflect their concept of Change as the one un-changing aspect of the universe normally perceptible to human beings. In this universal context individual changes are relatively unimportant; it is the process of change itself which needs to be emphasized.[5]

"Changes" in the translation "*Book of Changes*" means many assorted changes oc-curring here and there, but that is not what the *Yijing* (*I Ching*) is about. It is about the fundamental concept of "Change" and also presents a method for tracking the "process" (activity) of "change." In the translation "*Book of Change*," the meaning of "Change" includes both the concept and the process of change.[6]

In the modern view, shamans have often been suspected of using their powers to cause harm. Consequently, you may ask why I say that the ancient

---

3   Confucius. *LunYu (The Analects).* Chapter 7.
4   Shima, Qian. *Shiji: Zhuan (Biography) Siku Quanshu* (Four Reservoirs of Ancient Texts) 1773.
5   Blofeld, John. *I Ching* (New York: Arkana, 1991: 23–24).
6   Reid, Daniel. Email conversation with Zhongxian Wu.

Wu were enlightened beings. To answer this question, I think we need to discuss Wu and shamanism here, even though I discussed this in my book *Vital Breath of the Dao*.[7]

WU 巫: CHINESE SHAMANISM

Artifacts from the Peiligang 裴李崗, Hongshan 紅山, and Yangshao 仰韶 culture (5000–3000 BCE) indicate that Wu 巫 culture has existed for more than 8000 years of Chinese history. The levels of knowledge and mastery over the material and non-material elements of the world achieved by the Wu were indeed profound and were highly regarded throughout most of ancient China. All of the legendary sages and cultural heroes of China's proto-historical past possessed the remarkable superhuman attributes of the Wu. The ancient Chinese emperors were Wu, and through the ancient Chinese classics, we can understand the role of the Wu. In fact, many classics are named after great emperors or sages.

The treasure of unearthed oracle bones and other artifacts reveal that the Wu were most esteemed during China's Three Dynasties (Xia 夏, Shang 商, and Zhou 周) period (2100–256 BCE), which is when they achieved their greatest prominence. In his research into Shang Wu 商巫, archeological scholar Chen Mengjia identifies the king as a shaman:

> Some of the oracle bone inscriptions (used in ritual divination) state that the "king divined" or that "the king inquired in connection with wind"— or rainstorms, rituals, conquests, or hunts. There are also statements that "the king made the prognostication that...," pertaining to weather, the border regions, or misfortunes and diseases; the only prognosticator ever recorded in the oracle bone inscriptions was the king... In addition, inscriptions describing the king dancing to pray for rain and the king prognosticating about a dream are numerous. All of these were activities of both king and shaman, which indicate in effect that the king was a shaman.[8]

The Chinese character Wu 巫 can be used as a noun or an adjective and can be translated as shaman, shamanism, or shamanic. As discussed in my article, "*Drumming and Dancing: Feeling the Rhythm of Qigong, Calligraphy, and Wu*

---

7   Wu, Zhongxian. *Vital Breath of the Dao: Chinese Shamanic Tiger Qigong* (St Paul, MN: Dragon Door Publications, 2006: 81–100).

8   Chang, K.C. *Art, Myth, and Ritual: The Path to Political Authority in Ancient China* (Cambridge, MA: Harvard University Press, 1983: 45–47).

(Shamanism)",[9] the Chinese character Wu is commonly translated as shaman—a somewhat incomplete interpretation. The word shaman comes from the Tungusu-Manchurian language. The practice of a Wu only distantly resembles that of current day shamans, who travel in "alternative realities" as part of their religion. They are mostly located in Siberia and are very aggressive. In trance, but still in full possession of their faculties, these shamans may climb the World Tree to reach the "Heaven of the Ancestors" or descend to an underworld in search of lost or trapped souls. They undergo difficult and painful initiations, including ritual death and rebirth. In contrast, the Wu referred to by the Chinese character is much more of a spirit-medium. Through natural ability, training, and ritual preparation, the Wu can summon the bright spirits. These spirits inhabit and speak through the Wu's body.[10]

Shamans specialize in ritual and possess unique powers that enable them to act as intermediaries between humans and the shadowy world of spirits and the supernatural. However, the ancient Wu are not the same as modern-day shamans and are different from the modern concept of Wu. Today's Wu may channel transmissions from spirit bodies without being able to recall the communication. In ancient China, the Wu were omniscient and they governed the country in addition to aiding others in transcending the physical plane. They were also able to function as doctors and taught disease prevention. Their keen observation of and close relationship with the universe even enabled them to avert natural disasters. Indeed, the Wu possessed Shenming 神明 (literally "Spiritual Clarity" or "Spiritual Brightness"): Spiritual Enlightenment, and a deep understanding of the universal way. The Wu were enlightened beings who embodied Tian Ren He Yi 天人合一, the union of the human being and the universe. Through this ritual connection with Heaven, they sustained both Yin and Yang—stillness and movement.[11]

The Chinese character Wu 巫 carries a great deal of meaning. The common character for Wu is written as 巫, which contains the radical Gong 工 (work) and Ren 人 (person). It is an image of two people working together or of two shamans doing their ritual dance. The syllable Wu, written and intoned differently, also means dancing. It is no coincidence that dancing connects the Wu to the universe

---

9   Wu, Zhongxian. *"Dancing and Drumming—Feeling the 'Rhythm' of Qigong, Calligraphy, and Wu (Shamanism)." Qi-Journal*, Winter 2003–2004: 25.

10   Karcher, Stephen. *Ta Chuan* (New York: St Martin's Press, 2000: 40).

11   Li Zehou, *Jimao Wu Shuo* (Beijing: Zhongguo Dianying Chubanshe, 1999: 68).

and helps develop their Shenming. According to *Xici* 繫辭, as written in one of the *Ten Wings of the Yijing*,[12] we can achieve a full understanding of our own Shen 神 (spirit) and can communicate with high-level beings through dancing and drumming. Dancing and drumming are methods to help us understand the Shen. Even the shamans of today use the ritual of dancing to facilitate universal connections such as bringing rain to dry farmland. The ancient Wu were able to elevate their spirits to become one with all other spirits.

Similarly, in the Shang oracle bones, the Chinese character Wu is written with two of the same radicals for Gong 工, which means work or to work. Literally, this radical stands for a carpenter's square, a tool used for making squares (Fang 方). This is significant because in ancient Wu time, Gong, a carpenter's square, was the universal measurement, and it stood for order and correct behavior or the law of nature. Fuxi, who invented the *Yijing* Bagua (Eight Trigrams) and prediction system, holds the Gong as shown in some ancient scrolls. In the *Huangdi Neijing* (*Classic of Medicine*), Gong means doctor. Ancient Chinese medicine doctors were no different from Wu. They had the ability to help because they understood the way of the universe and the truth of life. Therefore, the original function of Wu was to connect with universal energy (or living in the Dao) and to pass on the universal knowledge to others.

WU 巫 AND CHINESE CULTURE

Wu depicts Sifang 四方—four directions or four quadrates (squares). Sifang can be translated as the four cardinal directions—north, south, east, and west. This is the pattern that the ancient Wu applied to the center of their bodies as "high-tech" equipment to communicate with the other four directions, and it was through this practice that they understood the universal way. This practice is called Zhongdao 中道 (Central Way) in Chinese. In this Wu tradition, the body is the central direction coordinated with the other four directions. Therefore, Sifang (four directions) includes the fifth direction—the center. These five directions in Fang are equal to the five elements in Chinese philosophy. My guess is that the five elements philosophy originated in this Wu function.

---

12 There are ten commentaries to the *Yijing*. It is commonly believed that Confucius wrote these commentaries to assist modern people in understanding the terse and cryptic language of the original text. Today, these are included with the *Yijing* and referred to as the "*Ten Wings*" because they assist our minds in understanding deeper meanings and thus help us achieve greater heights.

Fang

Wu

Commonly, Fang 方 means directions, method, place, square, and way. In Chinese oracle bones style writing, the character Fang is similar to the Wu. It looks like a person holding the Wu (shamanic) ruler and using it as a tool to measure the universe. Fang is the way that ancient Wu applied the tool to understand the universe. Fang also represents the cosmos. If you have the tool, you will understand the way. In traditional Chinese philosophy, we can use Fang to represent space and time. Actually, the ancient Chinese concept of the universe is related to space and time. The Chinese name for the universe is Yuzhou 宇宙. In *Huainanzi* 淮南子, the definitions of Yu are up, down, four directions (front, back, left, and right), and the definitions of Zhou are past, present, and future.[13]

Ancient Chinese Wu (shamans) created their cosmology through the Fang. From a Chinese Wu (shamanic) cosmological perspective, the universe—Fang—is constructed of three layers in space and time. In space, the layers are: upper layer, Tian (Heaven); lower layer, Di (Earth); and middle layer, Ren (Humanity). In time, the layers are past, present, and future. Human beings are a microcosm reflecting this macrocosm. Human beings are also constructed of three layers: Jing (Essence), Qi (Vital energy or life force), and Shen (Spirit). Each layer contains its own Fang. Therefore, in *Yijing* numerology science, the numbers three and five embody the way of the universe (three layers and five elements).

This Wu cosmological philosophy is fundamental to all Chinese traditions. Many aspects of Chinese culture (music, art, medicine, philosophy, etc.) are

---

13 Liu, An. *Huainanzi*, Chapter 1.

attributed to Wu, Chinese shamanism. For instance, in Chinese medicine, Fang stands for formula. Making a formula is Zufang 組方, which literally means organize directions/place and time. It hints that the ancient Wu understood through their bodies (the center) that different herbal formulas had different Universal Qi that was associated with different directions/places and time period. A Wu/doctor making a formula was the way to reorganize a patient's body (microcosm).

Confucianism and Daoism, the two main pillars of classical Chinese tradition, both originated in the ancient world of shamanism. As the way of humanity, Confucianism inherited and rationalized the knowledge of courtesy, ceremonial rites and regulations, and aspects of personal emotion from the ancient shamanic rituals. As the way of nature, Daoism rationalized and expanded the wisdom of the universal way and applied pragmatic knowledge from the ancient shamanic rituals.[14] *The Book of Change* is regarded as the most revered classic of Confucianism. It would be incorrect, however, to think that the *Yijing* is based solely on Confucianism, since Daoism contains most of the pragmatic methods of *Yijing* science, such as Chinese five elements astrology, *Fengshui,* and various divination methods.

Actually, Chinese medicine represents the joining of Daoism and Confucianism and is thoroughly based on *Yijing* science. The Tang 唐dynasty (617–907 CE) sage Sun Simiao 孙思邈, who is respected as the "Medical King" by the Chinese, stated that "nobody qualifies to be a master physician without knowledge of *Yijing*."[15] Confucius indicates in Chapter 13 of *Lunyu* 論語 (*Analects*) that "A person should not be a *Wu* (shaman) and/or doctor if he/she is without constancy [dedicated to the practice]." Indeed, Chinese medicine and Chinese shamanism are widely considered to have originated from the same source. In Chinese, the term is *Wu yi tong yuan* 巫医同源, which translates literally as "shaman doctor same source." In fact, many of the ancient documents verify that ancient Chinese doctors were ancient shamans.[16]

From this evidence, we can conclude that the *Wu* is the source of all classical Chinese traditions. Through their ability to communicate with nature, the ancient *Wu*—the enlightened beings—created the philosophy of the ancient Chinese cosmos that affected the whole of Chinese history and culture—and

---

14 Li Zehou. *Jimao Wushuo* (Beijing: Zhongguo Dianying Chubanshe, 1999: 65–66).

15 Zhang, Jiebing. "*Yi yi yi.*" *Leijing Fuyi* (Xian: Shaanxi Kexue Jishu Chubanshe, 1996: 350).

16 Chen, Lai. *Gudai Zongjiao yu Lunli—Rujia Shixiang de Genyuan* (Beijing: Sanlian Shudian, 1996: 35).

this cosmology became the fundamental elements of *Yijing* and its prediction systems.

THE SECRET OF *YIJING*

The *Yijing*, or *I Ching* (*The Book of Change*), is one of the most popular ancient Chinese classics in the West. We can find many published versions of the *Yijing* if we look in bookstores or search on the Internet. However, after taking a look at some of these books and communicating for more than five years with dedicated *Yijing* practitioners in America, I feel that some essential parts of the *Yijing* knowledge—the symbolism and numerology—have been missing for Westerners.

The Doorway of all Mystery

The *Yijing*, or *I Ching*, is a divination book that originates from the ancient Wu 巫 (ancient Chinese shamans or enlightened beings).

The *Yijing* contains three secret layers of wisdom: Xiang 象 (symbolism), Shu 數 (numerology), and Li 理 (philosophy). Since the *Yijing* is considered the root of ancient Chinese science and civilization, it can also be used to gain deep insights into the practice of Chinese medicine, spiritual cultivation, and our daily lives. However, if we want to attain the ancient knowledge of the *Yijing*, we have to master two things:

1. Number—We need to understand the transition from a number to a Gua 卦 (trigram or hexagram) because this is the key to the divination method.

2. Symbol—After we determine the Gua 卦 from the number, we need to understand the symbolic meaning of the Gua 卦 and its interpreting system.[17]

The high-level *Yijing* masters regarded the practical *Yijing* information on Xiang and Shu as the secret keys to the mystical gates of the universe and the human being. They believed that a person with high virtue who mastered these keys would bring great benefit to others. In contrast, they felt that a person with a big ego or without ethics who mastered the keys would bring much harm to others. Therefore, they always picked their students carefully and taught their complete knowledge to only a few specially chosen students. This holds true in other Chinese wisdom traditions as well:

"Don't teach someone if he or she is not the right person."

"Don't leak the secrets of the universe."

I have read these two sentences often in old texts on the *Yijing*, Chinese medicine, martial arts, and internal alchemy. Because Chinese masters have followed these admonitions, most Chinese people have no knowledge of Xiang and Shu. Although there are many different English versions of the *Yijing*, most of them just contain information on Li, the philosophical part of the *Yijing*, and it is therefore difficult for Westerners to find high-quality information about Xiang and Shu.

The spirit of the *Yijing* is about prediction and change. It is important to be attuned to universal energy and to listen within ourselves for guidance and direction in our daily lives and inner cultivation. We are living in an invisible, vivid

---

17 Li, Ling. *Zhongguo Fangshu Kao* (Beijing: Dongfang Chubanshe, 2000: 260).

universal Qi 氣 (energy) field; thus, sometimes we need to alter our plans if the energy changes. My original plan was to write a series of Chinese shamanic wisdom books in English that included some writing about the *Yijing*. I was planning to begin with a book entitled *The Way of Enlightenment: Chinese Shamanic 28 Lunar Mansions Cosmic Qigong*. However, after giving several workshops on *Yijing* divination techniques, healing, and spiritual cultivation, I received great inspiration from nature during my recent travels. Because of this, I changed my mind about the order of writing my books.

THE SPIRIT OF *YIJING*

Let me share with you an interesting *Yijing* prediction case from my September 2007 Lifelong Training session on the Oregon Coast even though you might be confused by the prediction details:

> As usual, we began our evening session at 8:00 p.m. Twenty-five of us were sitting in a circle to review the *Yijing* prediction practice. Before everyone had completely settled down, Jack said in an anxious voice, "I have the number 648." After doing the calculation, we got the corresponding trigram Kun/ Earth. "Your question might be related to Earth or southwest. What is your question?" one of the students asked. "I just got a phone call from my wife. She has spent hours looking for our dog but can't find him. We are very worried. Do you think we will be able to find him?" After considering the symbolic meanings of the trigram, everyone gave Jack advice.
>
> "The trigram Kun is related to the belly. The dog might have been hungry. Maybe he went in the southwest direction to find food. You should have your wife drive in that direction to look for the dog."
>
> "Since the prenatal location of southwest is the trigram Xun, the symbolic meaning of Xun is wind. This could represent the news on the air, so you should ask your wife to make an announcement on the local radio."
>
> "The dog should be on the southwest side of your house. Is the land flat on that side of your house?"
>
> After about a half hour of discussing this case, I said, "Your dog is definitely on the southwest side of your house. You should be able to find him. In fact, your wife might have found him already. Let's take a break and you can give your wife a call."

Jack was still sitting there looking at me with a worried look on his face after everyone had left for the break. I walked over to him and repeated, "Please call your wife. She might have found the dog already." He walked away with hesitating steps to make the call.

Everyone came back to the circle after the break. Jack was sitting there with a smile on his face. I said, "Jack, do you have good news to share with us?" Jack responded in a cheerful voice, "Yes, I do. My wife found our dog!" Everyone was excited. "We have a barn on the southwest side of our house," Jack continued. "There is a large piece of flat land on this side. Somehow, the dog got into the barn today and stayed inside. My wife looked in the barn this afternoon but didn't see him. While we were in the midst of our discussion, she checked the barn and found the dog inside."

This story demonstrates how we applied an ancient divination system in our prediction, which is different from what you see in other *Yijing* books. *Yijing* divination or prediction depends on the knowledge of Xiang (symbolism) and Shu (numerology) in the Bagua 八卦 (Eight Trigrams) of the *Yijing*. It goes back to the ancient *Yijing* divination schools. This old divination system does not check what the *Yijing* book says during the divination process because the lineage existed long before the book was written. This divination system is based on the *Yijing* knowledge of Xiang (symbolism) and Shu (numerology) in the Xiantian Bagua 先天八卦 (Prenatal Trigrams Arrangement) and Houtian Bagua 後天八卦 (Postnatal Trigrams Arrangement). We can find some of the knowledge in Confucius' *Shiyu* 十翼 (*Ten Wings*) and also in one of the oldest historical books, *Zuozhuan* 左傳. The Wu 巫 (Chinese shamanic) oral divination tradition holds some of the secret divination skills from this ancient system.

In this book, I will share the fundamentals of this ancient divination school. I will present this magical information as an eight-day course. After eight days of reading and studying *Seeking the Spirit of The Book of Change: 8 Days to Mastering a Shamanic Yijing (I Ching) Prediction System*, you should be able to master this essential *Yijing* prediction system. However, you should take your time and carefully study this book chapter by chapter; otherwise, you could easily get lost in this study, especially if you are not patient as you read the first four chapters.

In my experience, the great *Yijing* predictors always required their students to practice Qigong along with their *Yijing* study because Qigong is the essential foundation of *Yijing* prediction. Following this tradition, I will share a simple Taiji Qigong practice from the Hidden Immortals lineage at the end of each day's

Xiantian Bagua 先天八卦 *(Prenatal Trigrams Arrangement)*

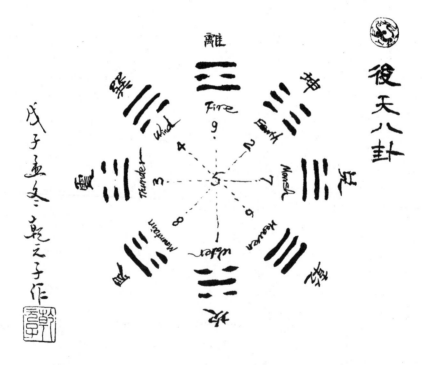

Houtian Bagua 後天八卦 *(Postnatal Trigrams Arrangement)*

training. You should practice these movements every day to support your inner cultivation while you are studying this *Yijing* prediction system.

One of the meanings of Yi 易 is easy, and the original *Yijing* prediction is easy to learn and easy to use. I hope this book will open a doorway for you to the mystical *Yijing* prediction systems.

QIAN 乾 —

DAY 1

Qian (heaven)

---

1   In Chinese tradition, we sometimes use trigrams to represent ordinal numbers; therefore, I use one of the Eight Trigrams as an ordinal number for each chapter in this book.

Dao (the way)

The spirit of tea is like the spirit of the Tao (Dao): it flows spontaneously, roaming here and there impatient of restraint.[2]

---

2   John Blofeld. *The Chinese Art of Tea* (Boston, MA: Shambhala Publications, 1985: ix).

1. Dao 道

The Way of Yi 易 and Tea

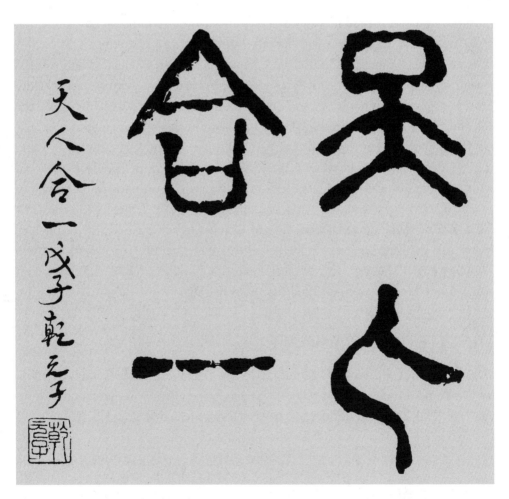

Tian Ren He Yi 天人合一 *(the union of the human being and the universe)*

Since the publication of my first Qigong book in English, *Vital Breath of the Dao: Chinese Shamanic Tiger Qigong* (February 2006), I have been enjoying my wandering Dao teaching style and experiencing different kinds of Qi 氣 (vital energy or breath) in nature. Qigong is a practice for cultivating inner knowledge and a method for moving into Tian Ren He Yi 天人合一 (the union of the human being and the universe). It is an ancient way of physical, mental, and spiritual cultivation. From the Qigong perspective, the body is a Qi (vital energy) network. One will maintain wellness if the Qi is free-flowing in this network. This ancient art for health maintenance, healing, and inner cultivation originated several thousand years ago in China. The Chinese tea ceremony is one of the high-level spiritual forms of Qigong, and the Gongfu/Kungfu 功夫[3] tea ceremony is a special and graceful tea ceremony. It is said that a Gongfu master invented it. Of course, I have shared my Gongfu tea ceremony with many friends during my travels.

Now six months later, it is autumn, in Bingxu 丙戌 (2006), the Fire Dog Year, and I am visiting mysterious Salt Spring Island in British Columbia. It is beautiful here in the autumn season. Autumn belongs to the Metal element and it is the season of change according to *Yijing* philosophy. Harmony requires the healthy process of change in nature as well as in the human body. When I first saw the colorful maple leaves decorating the entire island in this serene environment and my Lungs took in the fresh and transparent Qi (air) to rejuvenate my energy and spirit, I felt that I should write a book about the origin of *The Book of Change* with its divine prediction of change, so that we will be able to live in a state of peace and harmony. And also, Dog belongs to the Earth element and represents the doorway of the universe according to Chinese astrology. Earth gives birth to Metal, and the Metal element is my achievement element in terms of my Chinese astrology chart. Therefore, it is an auspicious time for me to have a cup of tea with you again to continue our spiritual path into the Dao.

THE CELESTIAL TEA HOUSE

Please send your spiritual body to my Celestial Tea House. Do you want to know how to do it? It is easy. Please relax your eyelids and close your eyes gently; bring your spiritual light (eyesight) back to your body; feel that you can see yourself

---

3   In Chinese, *Gongfu* means time. It also means a skill that is developed over a long time and through strenuous effort. This implies rigorous repetition of drills, both verbal and physical. *Gongfu* also means martial arts. See Wu, Zhongxian. *Vital Breath of the Dao: Chinese Shamanic Tiger Qigong* (St Paul, MN: Dragon Door Publications, 2006: 7).

with your inner eyes. Now, come into my tea house. I want to invite you to spend eight days with me in this tea house so that we will have many opportunities to follow the classical Chinese learning style, Pinming Lundao 品茗論道, which means "savor tea and discuss the Dao."

Let me show you around. As you can see, the tea house is located on the upper slope of a mountain. The tea house is eight-sided, an octagon with a "hemisphere roof" open to the sky. Before you enter the gate at the west side of the tea house, please turn around and look down the hill. You may have already noticed the small lake that lies at the foot of the hill and can be seen from the front of the tea house. The lake is quiet and its surface is like a mirror. We can see the reflection of the blue sky and the peaks upside down in the lake. Now, take a good look around.

Savor tea and discuss the Dao

39

From the northwest side of the tea house, we can see far away. The blue sky is clear and transparent. Occasionally, we can see some birds, such as eagles, flying above the trees. Far away in the distance, almost at the horizon, we can see a mountain ridge under the white clouds.

Let us turn to the north side and look up toward the top of the hill. We can see a high mountain peak touching the sky. The peak is covered with white snow. The snow is so bright that it makes us squint. To the northeast, we continue along the big mountain ridge covered with trees and notice the mist has risen, forming heavy clouds that obscure the top of the mountain.

Near the east side of the tea house are the cedar trees. You may notice some big burnt trunks, the result of past thunder and lightning storms. Shifting to the southeast side, just a few feet from the tea house, we see a bamboo garden. The breeze is kissing the bamboo and making the pleasurable sound of rustling leaves. It is as if we are listening to the waves on a sunny tropical beach.

On the south side of the tea house, sunlight makes the flowers so bright and colorful. Sparrows, hummingbirds, and other birds are visiting the flowers and trying to catch some worms for their meal. Then from the southwest side, we can see the land stretching far away. The farmland extends from the foot of the mountain; cows and buffalo are relaxing on the land. Now we come back to the west side of the tea house and enter inside.

This tea house is very special to me. I hope you will enjoy the visit. It is related to our topic about the *Yijing* and its Gua 卦. *Yijing* is also written as *I Ching* in English. Gua has been translated as trigram or hexagram in English, but it has many deep layers of meaning within. Come over here and let's have a cup of tea before we begin our discussion.

The tea table is on the south side of the tea house next to the window. From here, you can see the beautiful garden and the land. We will have our Gongfu tea ceremony now.

TEA CEREMONY

I put some hot water in the teapot and in the teacups to warm them up. Then I pour the water out into the tea tray. This is a special Gongfu tea tray, which has a holding compartment underneath to hold all the wastewater. This time, we will taste my formula for Gongfu tea, Double Dragon Plays with the Pearl.

First, I put some Green Dragon tea leaves in the bottom of the pot and add a Dragon Pearl tea ball on top of the Green Dragon. Next, I cover them with Black Dragon tea. Then, I pour boiling water into the teapot.

Tea tray

There are two small cups facing you on the tea table. One is a cylinder and the other one is a bowl. I am filling up your cylinder cup with the hot tea. Please cover it with the bowl cup for a minute. Be careful, it is hot. Now you can hold the cylinder cup with your middle finger and index finger, and the bowl cup with your thumb. Hold it stable and turn it over to place it on the tray. Very good! You did not leak any tea from your cups onto the tray. Are you ready for the tea? Please take a deep breath, then breathe out and imagine releasing all the old air/Qi from your body. Empty the body and hold—hold your breath, hold the empty state. Next, hold the cylinder and raise it gently, allowing the tea to flow into the bowl cup. Put the mouth of the empty cylinder cup right under your nose. Now take a deep breath from the cup to absorb the aroma down into your lower belly. Did you enjoy it? Yes, it is an enjoyable and relaxing experience.

Two cups

Hold the cup with three fingers

Wait a moment! Please do not drink this first cup of tea. It is for purification, and purification is one of the most important rituals in high-level Qigong and other Chinese spiritual cultivation traditions. The tea ceremony is one of the models for Qigong practice. We offer this first cup of tea as a sacrifice to nature. It also represents spiritual purification. I pour boiling water into the teapot again

Teapot with steam

and cover it with the lid. Now, let us pour the first cup of tea on the top of the teapot and observe what happens.

What do you notice? Yes, you can see the steam or mist rising from the surface of the teapot. Do you smell the expanding fragrance of the tea? Yes, you are feeling refreshed by breathing in the steam and fragrance. In Chinese, both steam and fragrance are *Qi.* We call steam, vapor, or mist Shuiqi 水氣 (water Qi) and fragrance Xiangqi 香氣 (perfume Qi). The steam from the tea reminds us that Qi originated in ancient Chinese shamanism. Offering sacrifice was an important way for ancient shamans to connect with high-level spirits or with their ancestors. The mist or vapor rising from a sacrificial offering was understood to be a pattern of mystery, connection, and communication between Heaven and human beings.

In the Afterword of *Vital Breath of the Dao*, I talked about the relationship between tea and Enlightenment. I said that I was going to talk about Enlightenment but in the beginning of today's discussion, I brought up the topic of *Yijing* first. What is the connection between *Yijing* and spiritual cultivation?

Yijing connects with spiritual cultivation. You will understand *Yijing* and its divination or prediction techniques at a deep level through your spiritual cultivation. On the other hand, you will improve your spiritual cultivation through your *Yijing* study.

You might wonder why I have spent so much energy talking about the tea. Often, these kinds of connections among different topics in the teachings of Chinese masters are not clear to Westerners. Sometimes, students ask me why I don't explain everything directly. In the way of Chinese wisdom tradition teaching, a master will not tell you everything directly. The master will help you find a way to discover your true understanding and Enlightenment on your own because you need to experience it yourself—and you have to be patient. It is like drinking the hot tea; we have to slow down and experience it. You will find that everything is connecting through savoring the tea slowly. Now, we can prepare to drink the next pot of tea.

THE SECRET OF THE UNIVERSE

I add hot water to the teapot and pour the tea into your cylinder cup again. You cover it with the bowl cup upside-down. We repeat this action, holding both cups firmly and turning them over. Smell the aroma from the cylinder cup. Now you can pick up your teacup with three fingers—thumb, index finger, and middle finger. These three fingers represent the trinity of the universe. Three is the creation number and stands for the way of nature.

Carefully observe the tea in this small cup. It is a pure, fresh, green color and it looks like a green crystal. The color gives me a peaceful feeling. Although it is a small cup of tea, do not swallow it all at once or it will hurt you. It is hot! Let your lips softly touch the edge of the cup.

Please take your first small sip of tea and hold it in your mouth. Taste it with the tip of your tongue. Take your second sip. Feel it on the coat of your

How to hold a tea cup

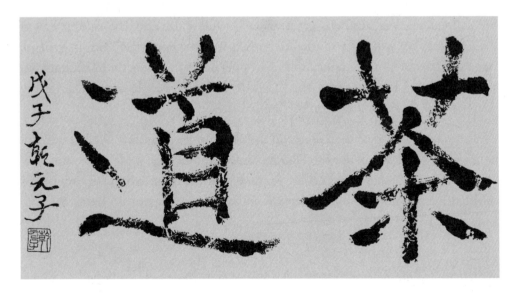

The Dao of tea 茶道

43

tongue. Then take your third sip and feel it with the root of your tongue. Can you feel the difference? Remember, you should take these three sips in one breath and swallow the tea slowly, feeling it pass through your throat and down into your Dantian 丹田.[4] This process is called Pin 品 in Chinese. The literal English translation of Pin is to taste or savor, but this does not convey its deeper meaning. In classical Chinese culture, Pin is also the way of study and the achievement of Enlightenment. This is a way of classical Chinese spiritual cultivation that we call Chadao 茶道 (the Dao of tea). It will help us understand the Dao (the way of the universe) if we know how to Pin (savor) the tea, because Pin holds the secret of the universe.

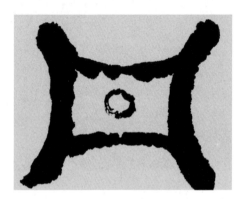

Dan (elixir)

What is the secret of the universe? Is this secret related to our daily life? The secret of the universe is the Dao, or way of the universe. The universe always exists in its own way, or law. As a microcosm of this macrocosm, each individual being is affected by this universal law. Actually, the universe does not hold any secrets from us. It becomes secret to most of us only because we do not understand it. Our daily life is connected with this secret of the universe. We will feel that everything is great when we follow the Dao, the natural way of the universe. We will suffer difficulties when we go against the Dao. In general, we are not aware of this connection. This phenomenon is exactly like Confucius states, "Bai xing ri yong er bu zhi 百姓日用而不知—People use it (Dao) every day, but they do not understand it (Dao)."[5]

Is it important for us to understand the secret of the universe? Well, it will not be important to learn about the Dao for those who do not want to change their life patterns—whether good or not so good. But for those who care about their spiritual life and are willing to lift their spirits, it will be good to know the Dao and to live with the Dao.

---

4   Dantian literally means elixir field and is located in the lower belly. Its function is to store the life force.

5   *Yijing. Xici (Appended Statements).* See *Zhouyi Shangshixue* (Beijing: Zhonghua Shuju, 1988: 291).

How can we become aware of this connection with the Dao in daily life? Fortunately, we have many ways to help wake up our consciousness to the Dao. For instance, at this moment, we are drinking tea, and Pin (savoring) the tea can serve as an example here. If we pick up the teacup and just swallow the tea without paying any attention to the tea, then drinking the tea will be meaningless to us. With heartfelt observation during our tea drinking, we can learn the Dao of tea, including the knowledge of the tea, the healing and cultivation functions of the tea, and the philosophy behind the drinking of tea. Therefore, three meanings are hidden within the Chinese character Pin (savor): Pinshu 品數 (quantity), Pinzhi 品質 (quality), and Chanpin 產品 (product). Let us have another cup of tea.

Qi (vital breath or energy)

TEA AND THE DAO 道

This cup of tea reminds me of John Blofeld's commentary on the art of tea:

> If one happens to have no interest in philosophical or metaphysical matters, talking learnedly about them while drinking tea becomes ridiculous. On the other hand, those who like that sort of thing may be gladdened by the reflection that the art of tea, like most traditional Chinese arts, involves harmony among the three powers—heaven, earth, and man.[6]

Dao is the way of the universe and it is always hidden within daily life. It expresses in different patterns in each moment in nature and in our lives. When most people drink tea, they are not aware that some meaningful universal secret

---

6   Blofeld, John. *The Chinese Art of Tea* (Boston, MA: Shambhala Publications, 1985: ix).

is hidden within the drinking pattern. Drinking is not merely drinking. As our hearts connect with the tea during the drinking, it becomes a much different experience. This is the spirit of the tea.

According to the Wu 巫 (ancient Chinese shamanic traditions), the universe has three layers: Heaven, Earth, and human being. Although tea is a small part of the universe, it holds the three powers. In each environment where it grows, the tea gathers different Heavenly Qi and Earthly Qi, and with different people processing it, the tea contains the Qi of different human beings. These are the reasons that we have different qualities of tea.

We may experience more of the trinity hidden within the tea when we drink it with more awareness. When I connect to the color of the tea with my eyesight, I feel it calms me down and makes me feel peaceful. This is the Heavenly power of tea. Eyesight represents the Shen 神 or spirit of the body, and in Wu traditions, the spirit is the Heaven layer of the body. When I absorb the aroma of the tea with my breath, I can feel it nourishing and purifying my five organ systems. This is the human being power of tea. Breath represents the Qi or vital energy of the body and the Qi is the human being layer of the body according to Wu. When I finally drink the tea with my mouth, I feel it as moist and smooth in my whole body and it makes me feel relaxed. This is the Earthly power of the tea. Mouth represents the Jing 精, or essence of the body, and Jing is the Earthly layer of the body according to Wu.

Shen 神 (spirit)

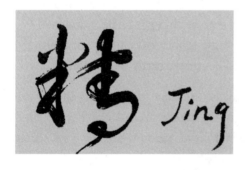

Jing 精 (essence)

Do you remember how many sips of tea we need to take in the Pin process? Yes, three sips. The number three stands for the Dao as the way of trinity. Trinity is one of the most important concepts in the Chinese shamanic spiritual traditions. Everything is constructed of the three layers. To understand the number three is another way to understand the Dao. For instance, in Qigong 氣功 practice, we always work with three: posture, breath, and visualization. This is the way to strengthen and harmonize the three treasures of the body: Jing (essence), Qi (vital energy), and Shen (spirit). This is no coincidence and it is why the *Yijing* uses three lines to construct a Gua (trigram). Each line represents a layer of the universe. Let us now explore some details of the Gua.

GUA 卦 (TRIGRAM OR HEXAGRAM)

As I discussed in *Vital Breath of the Dao*, "The original function of the Chinese characters was not merely to serve as a means of communication; rather, the characters were intended to serve as a vehicle for channeling universal wisdom and for connecting with nature."[7] It will be very helpful for understanding the *Yijing* book if we first construe the original meanings of the Chinese character Gua.

The whole text of the *Yijing* contains only 64 different Gua, or hexagrams. Although each hexagram has a different name, we refer to any hexagram as Gua when we talk about it. I believe the Chinese character Gua carries the spirit of the *Yijing*.

The way we study the deep meanings of Chinese characters, especially those in the ancient classics, is similar to the way we taste the tea. When we drink the tea, we need to slow down and feel the different kinds of energy in each small sip of tea with different parts of the mouth and the heart. When we try to gain insight into the flavor of Chinese characters, we need to follow in the footsteps of the ancient sages who invented these characters. For instance, as we check the dictionary for the meaning of Gua, it might say "symbols used in ancient divination;"[8] yet we may find a much more interesting meaning hidden within the character itself. Let us take three sips of tea and Pin Gua—study the deep meanings of the Chinese character Gua.

The Chinese character Gua 卦 is made of the left radical Gui 圭 and the right radical Bu 卜. Most Chinese dictionaries will give the meaning of the Chinese character Gui as "a jade tablet with a square base and a triangle top used in official

---

7   Wu, Zhongxian. *Vital Breath of the Dao: Chinese Shamanic Tiger Qigong* (St Paul, MN: Dragon Door Publications, 2006: 9).

8   *Hanyu Dazidian* (*The Great Dictionary of Chinese*) (Chengdu: Sichuang Cishu Chubanshe, 1996: 44).

Gui

Bu—a pattern of cracks

ceremonies in ancient China," but dictionaries will not tell you why a Gui was needed in ancient ceremonies and why it was made of jade with a square base and a triangle on top. The original meaning of Gui may give us some indications. Gui is related to territory. It has the meanings of measurement, sundial, and platform. This character is made with two of the same radical Tu (earth or clay) on the top and on the bottom. It is the pattern of an earth platform, and it is the place where the Wu (ancient Chinese shamans) observed the universe or performed their spiritual rituals to connect with the universal energy.

The function of Gui is to connect or communicate with the ancestral spirits or nature spirits during an official ceremony. The ancient Chinese shamans understood that good-quality jade could hold high-quality Qi or spiritual energy and they used many different types of jade ritual objects during their ceremonies. The square base of a Gui represents Earth and stability. The triangle top of a Gui represents the trinity or three powers of Heaven or the universe. Therefore, it stands for the harmony within Heaven, Earth, and the human being.

We should understand that a Gua (trigram or hexagram) holds the spiritual connection with Heaven, Earth, and the human being through the above information about Gui.

The Chinese character Bu means divination or to divine. Bu 卜 looks like a pattern of cracks and is also related to two pieces of animal horn. Before the Zhou 周 dynasty (1027–256 BCE), ancient Chinese shamans used two forms of Bu to do the divi-nation. These two forms are Rebu 熱 卜 (hot-style divination) and Lengbu 冷卜 (cold-style divination). Numerous unearthed oracle bones indicate that Rebu played the main role in Shang 商 dynasty (1600–1027 BCE) divination. No one knows the details of the Rebu divination skills now. But some Lengbu divination techniques are still alive in certain rural areas of southern China.

During a Rebu divination process, the Wu would burn a scapula bone or tortoise shell. The bone or shell would break during burning, and a pattern of cracks would appear. The shaman could get an answer to the question through the pattern of cracks. The pronuncia-

Bu—two pieces of animal horn

tion of Bu is related to divination as well. The moment the bone or shell cracked in the fire, it made the noise Bu. Therefore, the moment the shaman heard the sound of Bu, he got the pattern that was the answer for the divination.[9] This rela-tionship between the divination and the pronunciation of Bu also appears in the Lengbu divination process.

During a Lengbu divination process, the Wu (shaman) placed two pieces of horn halves in front of him, then burned incense and prayed for answers to his questions. Next, the shaman picked up the horn halves and threw them on the ground. The moment the horns hit the ground, they made the Bu noise and revealed a pattern. The shaman could get an answer to his questions from this pattern.

Actually, almost none of the methods for *Yijing* divination described in the *Yijing* books on the market are about Bu. Those other methods are related to an-other Chinese character: Shi 筮. This Shi divination was developed in the Zhou dynasty and this method has been passed down to us over 3000 years. The Chinese character Shi 筮 is made of the top radical Zhu 竹 and the bottom

---

9   Wu, Zhongxian. *Vital Breath of the Dao: Chinese Shamanic Tiger Qigong* (St Paul: Dragon Door Publications, 2006: 11).

radical Wu 巫. Zhu means bamboo and it represents things made from bamboo or grass. Wu means shaman and it also represents a predictor. Therefore, Shi literally means a shaman who uses bamboo sticks or yarrow sticks as tools to do a prediction. In general, we call *Yijing* divination Bushi 卜筮.

The original meaning of Gua (trigram) is to decode the answer through divination. Some ancient *Yijing* scholars interpret Gua 卦 as another Chinese character: Gua 挂, which means to hang. In other words, it means each Gua in the *Yijing* is like a picture hanging on the wall so that we can see it very clearly. And it hints that a clear answer appears in a Gua in response to the question posed in the *Yijing* divination.

Through Pin (studying) the meanings of the Chinese character Gua, we can tell that *Yijing* is a divination book from the Wu (ancient Chinese shamans). Before you leave today's discussion, I want to invite you to do a Taiji Qigong movement with me. I believe that this practice will help you get a clear answer in your future divination.

TAIJI QIGONG QIAN 乾 (HEAVEN)

It is late in the afternoon on a beautiful autumn day and the sun decorates the entire land with its golden-yellow light. Let us face the northwest direction so that we can enjoy the pure and colorful Heavenly Qi. Now, let us practice the Qian movement.

Movement: Stand with your feet parallel, shoulder-width apart and toes grabbing the Earth. Straighten your back so it is solid like a mountain. Lift your perineum to seal the Dihu 地户 (Earthly Door, acupuncture point CV1). Pull your lower abdomen in. Open your chest. Straighten your neck and keep your head upright. Imagine your head touching Heaven with the Tianmen 天門 (Heavenly Gate, acupuncture point GV20) open. Put the tip of your tongue on the tooth ridge behind your teeth. Close your teeth and mouth. Keep your shoulders down, arms relaxed, and armpits open. Open your hands with fingers straight. Close your eyes with eyelids relaxed. Take your eyesight within. Listen within. Breathe through your nose and your skin. Adjust your breathing to be slow, smooth, deep, and even. There should be no noise from your breathing. In Chinese, this breathing technique is called *Mimi Mianmian* 密密綿綿, meaning the breathing is soft and unbroken like cotton and silk (Figure 1).

Visualization: With your eyes closed, look and listen within to your body. Feel your body split from your waist, with your upper body suspended and your lower body rooted into the Earth. Feel the Heavenly Qi penetrate through the Tianmen down to the Dantian as you inhale. Imagine the Qi moving down from your Dantian 丹田 through your legs and rooting into the Earth as you exhale. Feel your body relax, standing like a pine tree.

Function: This movement appears to do nothing, but it is doing a great deal because it is a way to help you awaken your consciousness, your original life source, and it is creating and nourishing your life force. This movement opens the body and enables us to connect with the universal Qi. It helps us learn about the union of the physical body and the spiritual body. Daily practice of this movement strengthens the vital energy and is good for rebuilding one's life energy from a state of weakness. It also awakens your spirits. This is the spiritual foundation of *Yijing* prediction.

Now you can rest in the guest room on the northwest side of the tea house. I hope you will enjoy the Qi there. I will see you tomorrow.

Figure 1

51

Wuwei (actionless)

DUI 兌

DAY 2

Dui (marsh)

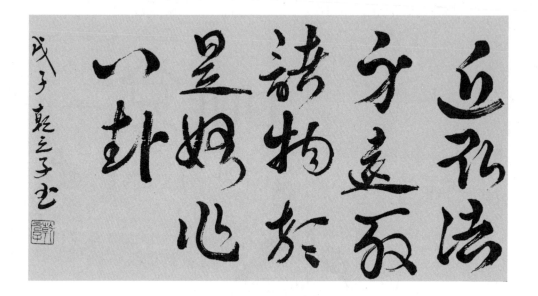

Jin qu zhu shen, yuan qu zhu wu, yu shi shi zuo Bagua.
近取諸身遠取諸物於是始作八卦
Near at hand, he learned each part of his body
and at a distance, he understood everything in nature;
then Fuxi 包犧 *invented Bagua* 八卦 *(Eight Trigrams)*[1]

---

1   *Yijing. Xici (Appended Statements)*. See *Zhouyi Shangshixue* (Beijing: Zhonghua Shuju, 1988: 307).

2. Yi 易

The Change and Myths

Yi (change)

Shenhua (myths)

In Chinese, Shen 神 means spirit, infinite, magic, marvelous, deity, and divine. Another meaning is to stretch, because ancient Chinese shamans may have performed stretching exercises to wake up their inner spirits or to invite the spirits of nature and ancestors. Actually, in the oldest written Chinese characters, the oracle bones style, the Chinese character for Shen is the same as the Chinese character for lightning. This means that lightning is related to the spirit of nature and is a message from Heaven. Hua 話 means speak, talk, tell, speech, and story. Literally, Shenhua 神話 means the story about spirits or gods, and it also means Chinese myths or mythology. There were many ancient Shenhua (myths) in Chinese shamanism. Actually, Shenhua is a doorway to the divine, and the deities in a myth are a reflection of different levels of consciousness or spirits.[2] Shenhua is also an entryway into the mystery of the *Yijing*.

A STORY OF CREATION AND GUA 卦 (TRIGRAM)

I hope you had a good sleep last night. That northwest corner guest room has special transparent Qi. Most people say that their breath feels smoother and deeper when they meditate in that room, and I have even felt all the pores of my skin moving with my breath when I have meditated there.

I have made a new tea formula for us today, chrysanthemum with the Yunwu 雲霧 (Clouds and Mist) green tea from my hometown area in southeast China. In general, I don't like to have the fragrance of flowers in my traditional Chinese tea. I prefer the original flavor and aroma of the tea. Chrysanthemum is the only flower that I occasionally choose to mix with my tea because this flower has good purity Qi which will be good for your Lungs, your breath, and your energy circulation.

---

2   Wu, Zhongxian. *Vital Breath of the Dao: Chinese Shamanic Tiger Qigong* (St Paul, MN: Dragon Door Publications, 2006: 46).

The hot tea always slows down our discussion, but it is a good way to enjoy the tea and our conversation. Let us have a cup of tea first. Are you ready for the adventurous path to the mystery of the ancient *Yijing*? Let's start with a creation story. I hope this story will help us gain better insight into the Gua. With three sips of the tea, we can begin the story.

In the beginning of the universe, there was nothing but one mass of Qi, and this Qi was moving chaotically within the mass. In Chinese, this mass of Qi is called Hundun 混沌, which means chaos. This mass was shaped like an egg. It was dark, as if it had a black hole or cave within it. After millions of years, the different qualities of Qi within the mass started moving in certain directions. The light and clear Qi started ascending, and it looked like the white of an egg; the heavy and turbid Qi started descending, and it looked like the yolk of an egg. After more millions of years, the ascending Qi formed Heaven and the descending Qi formed Earth. The Heavenly Qi and Earthly Qi were attracted to each other because they originated from the same mass, Hundun. So, after many more millions of years, through their interaction, the Heavenly Qi and Earthly Qi gave birth to all beings. The human being is the most treasured among them and represents all beings.

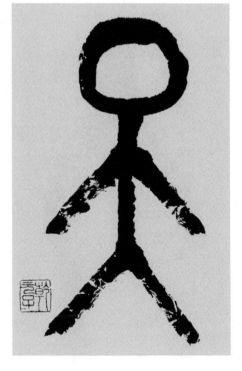

This story comes from Chinese shamanism. From a Chinese Wu (shamanic) cosmological perspective, the universe is based on the number three. The universe is constructed of three layers in space and time. In space, the layers are: upper layer, Tian 天 (Heaven); lower layer, Di 地 (Earth); and middle layer, Ren 人 (humanity or human being). In time, the layers are past, present, and future.[3] Human beings are a microcosm

Tian 天 (heaven)

---

3   Wu, Zhongxian. *Vital Breath of the Dao: Chinese Shamanic Tiger Qigong* (St Paul, MN: Dragon Door Publications, 2006: 87).

Di 地 *(earth)*

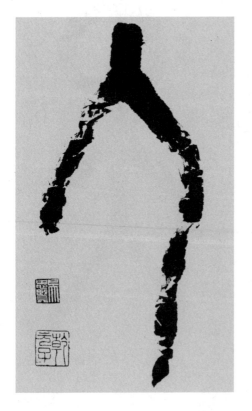

Ren 人 *(human being)*

reflecting this macrocosm. Human beings are also constructed of three layers: Jing 精 (essence), Qi 氣 (vital energy or life force), and Shen 神 (spirit) at the energetic level, or upper body, middle body, and lower body at the physical level. Each layer contains its own three cosmic layers.

This knowledge came from the Wu (ancient Chinese shamans) through their observations of nature, observing the way. They were able to see everything from the parts of the body, the internal world. This means that they observed their own bodies and, through their bodies, they were able to understand the interconnectedness of everything and the reason for the existence of everything. Looking through the universe of your own body is the same as looking at the totality of the universe. Nature has a way of ordering everything in this way.

In the science of *Yijing* numerology, the number three embodies the way of the universe. Each Gua, or trigram, is made with three lines. The top line represents the Heavenly way, the bottom line represents the Earthly way, and the middle line represents the human being way between Heaven and Earth. Everything is a unit of the trinity; therefore, we can find that everything is related to one of the Gua.

Yidao 易道 *(way of change)*

TEA AND YI 易 (DIVINATION)

We can use different Gua to represent different things. When we drink tea, the tea is related to a Gua. In general, the tea leaves belong to the Xun 巽 Gua (the trigram that represents Wind). But the Gua would be different if we determined a Gua from a different kind of tea because the energy would be different. For instance, the pure green color of the Double Dragon Plays with the Pearl tea indicates the tea is related to Zhen 震 Gua (the trigram that represents Thunder).

You may wonder why the tea and the tea leaves have different Gua 卦. It is because the Qi (energy) of the tea leaves is different from the Qi of the liquid tea. The quality of the tea leaves is that they hold the energy of Heaven (climate), Earth (environment), and the human being (processing). When we make the tea, we put our energy into combining the tea leaves with the hot water, which then interact to create a new type of Qi. When different people make tea using the same tea leaves and hot water, there may be a big difference in the taste of the tea. Therefore, the Gua will be different for the tea made by each person.

This is an interesting part of the *Yijing*. The spirit of *Yijing* is change, which means you can never mechanically identify different Gua for the different objects. Actually, the identification of a Gua is the foundation of *Yijing* divination. It will be easy for us to learn how to make out a Gua from different things if we have some fundamental knowledge of *Yijing*. We will discuss the details later.

Going into nature is the best way to improve your knowledge of the *Yijing* and its Gua (trigrams). I understood the *Yijing* trigrams better with each moment I was in nature. For instance, every morning right before dawn, I jumped into Cusheon Lake during my BC Canada visit. I sensed the lake water energy to be like ice and crystals penetrating into my body through all the pores of my skin. I felt my body melting into the lake and becoming part of the lake. When I saw that the lake changed her face in each moment, I was experiencing the Wu (ancient Chinese shamans) reading the mystery of nature. The lake corresponds to the *Yijing* trigram Dui 兌. Each trigram has many aspects or meaning and Dui is lake, Dui is Metal, Dui is mouth, Dui is a beautiful teenage girl, Dui is joy, Dui is west, Dui is goat, and Dui is shaman. Through the lake, I appreciated that each trigram has many symbolic meanings or patterns, and I knew that there must be an energetic connection among all of the trigrams.

Now I'll make another pot of tea with the same tea leaves in the teapot. The aroma continues to rise from the tea and the tea color has changed to a deeper green. Let us drink the tea to learn more about the *Yijing*.

The spirit of *Yijing* is about Yi 易. The original meaning of Yi is divination or predict. In general, Yi 易 is translated as "change" in English. In old *Yijing* 易經 divination schools, the divination technique is flexible and not at all mechanical. Please be aware that the flexibility of the divination skill does not mean that you can freely make up your own way. In fact, the divination method itself embodies the three layers of meaning of Yi, the Change: Buyi 不易 (No Change), Bianyi 變易 (Change), and Jianyi 簡易 (Simple Change). Let us take a look at these layers.

The first layer of meaning of Yi is "No Change" and it represents that the Dao is always there and never changes its way. In the divination, it means that we will never change the rules of the divination and that we must follow the rules. This is similar to the tea. No matter how many different kinds of tea leaves from different areas we use to make our tea, we still call all of them tea.

Cusheon Lake

The second layer of meaning of Yi is "Change" and it represents that the Dao expresses its way in different patterns in nature and in our daily lives. In divination, it means we can use different techniques to do the divination, and we should understand that the same Gua in different situations should be interpreted for different meanings.

Do you notice the change in the different sips of tea? This is the same tea, but we can notice a difference from sip to sip and from cup to cup. These differentiations symbolize the subtlety of nature. The subtlety is an expression of the Dao; the subtlety is an expression of the universe; and the subtlety is an expression of the Yidao 易道 (way of change).

The third layer of meaning of Yi is "Simple Change" and it represents that although the Dao expresses its way in different patterns, we can learn about this through vigilant observation. Through Simple Change, we can see the different patterns in the same object to gain insight about the change. Yi also means that the way of *Yijing* is simple and easy. In divination, we should catch the Simple Changes during the *Yijing* consultation to help us decode the answer. This should be easy to do. Now, let me share one of my experiences with you.

The moment the ferry left Fulford Harbor on Salt Spring Island, BC Canada, I was standing on the deck with my friends and enjoying my last view of the island's magnificence. As I looked back at Mt. Maxwell, nature showed her magic to me again. The Earthly Qi rose from the island in the form of a cloud. In just a few minutes, it formed into a bald eagle. I quickly took out my camera and recorded that moment. The eagle was playing with its shamanic power and in just a few seconds, it changed into a huge tree to connect with Heaven and Earth. At that moment, I was aware of what the spirit of *Yijing* is.

Yijing is about Yi (Change). It is essentially about the phenomenon, the idea, and the process of change as the basic dynamic of the universe. Let's go back to the cloud pattern. What will we learn from this cloud in our *Yijing* study? No matter what pattern a cloud forms, we still call it a cloud. This is the meaning of No Change and it represents that the Dao is always there and never changes its way. The meaning of Change can be seen in the cloud pattern changing from an eagle into a tree, which demonstrates that the Dao expresses its way in different patterns in nature and in our daily lives. Although the cloud changed into different patterns, we can still recognize it as the pattern of an eagle or a tree. This is the meaning of Simple Change. It represents that although the

Eagle

Tree

Dao expresses its way in different patterns, we can learn about this through our vigilant observation.

From a *Yijing* numerology perspective, the three layers of Change are known as Han San He Yi 含三合一, which means holding Three in One. Chinese ancient Wu 巫 (shamans) understood that three is the universal creation number. Trinity is one of the most important concepts in the Chinese shamanic spiritual traditions.[4] Yi 易 (Change) is the expression of the Dao; it is the number one, Yi 一 in Chinese. The three layers of Change are represented by the number three, San 三 in Chinese. In the *Yijing*, one trigram is made up of three lines; to understand the number three is another way to understand Yi (Change), and the Dao.

Let us try another sip of the tea. This sip of tea may help us grasp the meaning of the Simple Change. I taste the tea with the tip of my tongue and notice the flavor is a little bitter. I taste the tea again with the coat of my tongue and the aroma spreads in my mouth. As I send the tea through my throat down to my Dantian, I feel the sweet flavor swirling in my throat. Then my mouth is full of the sweet lingering taste as if I had drunk the juice of a honeydew melon. This is Simple Change! This experience of a sip of tea confirms my spiritual cultivation path: from bitter to sweet. Is life patterning the same as this sip of tea? What is your experience of this sip of tea?

FUXI 伏羲: THE FIRST CHINESE SHAMAN KING

We have another sip of tea and meditate on it. After a few minutes, I take out a Chinese *Yijing* book to share some information with you. In the *Yijing* book, *Xici* 繫辭 describes Fuxi 包犧, who invented the Bagua (Eight Trigrams) through his observation of his own body, other beings, and the patterns of nature.

Xici is one of the most important old *Yijing* commentaries, and it literally means "Appended Statements." There are ten commentaries to the *Yijing*. It is commonly believed that Confucius wrote them to assist people in understanding the terse and cryptic language of the original text. Today, these are included with the text of the *Yijing* and are referred to as the "*Ten Wings*" because they assist our minds in understanding the deeper meanings and thus help us achieve greater heights. In other words, we could not "fly" (reach the high level) to the *Yijing* knowledge without the *Ten Wings*. *Xici* is one of the *Ten Wings*.

---

4   Wu, Zhongxian. *Vital Breath of the Dao: Chinese Shamanic Tiger Qigong* (St Paul, MN: Dragon Door Publications, 2006: 41).

Fuxi is one of the oldest shaman kings in ancient China. His name was written in a different way in some documents because Chinese is a very complicated language system. The same Chinese character may be pronounced in a totally different way in different regions of China. For instance, the Chinese character for tea 茶 is pronounced Cha by the northern Chinese; in my hometown in southeast China, we pronounce it Tei; and in most parts of my home province, people pronounce it Sho. The same Chinese character may have many meanings and different regions may use different Chinese characters to represent the same object. In some documents, Fuxi is written as Baoxi.

Fuxi is the original ancestor of the human being according to many Chinese myths. Here is one common version of these myths from different tribes in China:

> Long, long ago, a huge flood occurred in the world. It destroyed everything and killed almost all beings, but a boy named Fuxi and a girl named Nuwa 女媧 were hidden inside a Hulu 葫蘆 (gourd). This Hulu floated on the water for many days. After the flood, the boy and girl came out of the Hulu. They were the only human beings who survived the flood. Later, they got married and gave birth to many human beings. They became the first ancestors of the human beings.

Some scholars believe that the names Fuxi and Nuwa actually have the same meaning as Hulu because they had the same or a similar pronunciation in ancient China. Nuwa is the Yin 陰 perspective of Hulu or Fuxi.[5] In the Daoist traditions, Hulu is considered a symbol for the Dao. This story tells us one of the important

Fuxi and Nuwa

---

5   Wen, YiDuo 聞一多. *Wen YiDuo QuanJi* (Shanghai: KaiMing ShuDian, 1948: 59–60).

patterns of the Dao: the Dao generates the Yinqi 陰氣 and Yangqi 陽氣. It also reminds me of one *Yijing* divination of the Dao: "The combination of one Yin and one Yang is the Dao."[6] Fuxi (or Nuwa) is not merely a person; it is a symbol that represents the Dao and ancient Chinese civilization. Therefore, many old Chinese documents record that Fuxi, besides being the inventor of the Bagua 八卦, invented many other things and was the first to teach people some of the necessary life skills. He is credited with naming and taming animals, riding horses, making fire, cooking food, and many other things. He invented the fishing net, hunting, rule and law, the Qin 琴 and other musical instruments, mathematics, Chinese characters, the calendar, and the city, among other things.

Hulu 葫蘆 *(gourd)*

Through his careful observations of nature, Fuxi learned how to categorize different things. He understood that the best way to classify different objects was to use the number system because the abstract quality of a number could help to sort out the differences among the objects. For instance, each trigram has countless layers of symbolic meanings but each trigram is made up of only three lines. The most important thing is that Fuxi determined that the binary system is the basis of nature, and he invented the Bagua 八卦 (Eight Trigrams system) to represent the way of nature according to the binary system. Interestingly, when the philosopher Gottfried Wilhelm Leibniz (1646–1716 CE) examined Fuxi's Bagua arrangement, what he saw upon substituting a zero for each Yin line and a one for each Yang line was that Fuxi's arrangement represented a perfect binary numbering sequence. This helped him discover the binary system, which is the foundation of virtually all modern computer architectures.[7]

---

6   *Yijing. Xici (Appended Statements)*. See *Zhouyi Shangshixue* (Beijing: Zhonghua Shuju, 1988: 291).

7   See James A. Ryan. "Leibniz' Binary System and Shao Yong's Yijing." *Philosophy East & West*, Vol. 46, 1996: 59.

Qin 琴

The Bagua has two different arrangements. They are Xiantian Bagua (Prenatal Trigrams Arrangement) and Houtian Bagua (Postnatal Trigrams Arrangement). I think these two different arrangements represent different stages of the cosmos, a person, or an object.

BAGUA 八卦: THE EIGHT TRIGRAMS ARRANGEMENTS

Bagua is the model of the universe and everything in existence, including every part of the body, belongs to one of the trigrams. Ancient shamans understood this connection and they brought this connection into their interpretations of their divinations. We have to value this if we study *Yijing* philosophy and divination techniques because this connection is fundamental to the old divination school of *Yijing*. The Bagua is made with Eight Trigrams: Qian 乾 (Heaven), Dui 兌 (Marsh or Lake), Li 離 (Fire), Zhen 震 (Thunder), Xun 巽 (Wind), Kan 坎 (Water), Gen 艮 (Mountain), and Kun 坤 (Earth). Each line in a trigram will be either a solid line (—) or a broken line (--). The solid line is called the Yang 陽 line and the broken line is called the Yin 陰 line. Yin-Yang 陰陽 is one of the most important concepts in Chinese culture. We will discuss Yin-Yang later. Let us continue to focus on the Bagua for now.

Fuxi invented the Bagua to help others learn the universal way. I think it will help us to understand why the Bagua has two different arrangements if we first take a look at a cosmic myth:

Everything has its imperfections, the same as Heaven and Earth. Therefore, in ancient times, Nuwa refined five colored rocks to fix those imperfections. She cut off the feet of the Giant Turtle to make the four pillars to support Heaven and Earth. Later, two leaders from different tribes,

Gonggong 共工 and Zhuanxu 顓頊, fought for the position of emperor of China. Gonggong hit Buzhou 不周 Mountain and broke the Heavenly pillars and Earthly supports, which made Heaven lean to the northwest, and the sun, moon, and stars moved toward that space. The Earth lowered to the southeast and all the rivers and the water system flowed downward in that direction.[8]

From this story, we can see an ancient Chinese cosmos: in ancient times, Heaven above and Earth below were in an upright position and the axis of the Earth was vertical. Somehow, the universal energy made a dramatic change and Heaven shifted to the northwest and the Earth was broken in the southeast, so the axis of the Earth has been tilted ever since.

This story may not seem to make much sense to you. It made no sense to me when I first read it. Since this story is from China, we should link it to Chinese geography. I understood the story after I had traveled around to many places in China. Northwestern China is a high-altitude area, so you would have the feeling that Heaven is leaning on the Earth if you lived in that area. But at the edge of southeastern China, you could see only the ocean and, of course, rivers run to the ocean.

This story is related to the time period in which Nuwa lived. It was the same time period in which Fuxi invented the Bagua. The shifts of Heaven and Earth in the story indicate that the two different arrangements of the Bagua are the symbols of the cosmos before and after the shift.

I make a new pot of tea. We sip the new tea and then I open my Chinese *Yijing* book again. In the *Yijing Shuogua* 說卦 (one of the *Ten Wings*), we will discover some details of these two arrangements of the Bagua, Xiantian Bagua (Prenatal Eight Trigrams Arrangement) and Houtian Bagua (Postnatal Eight Trigrams Arrangement).

Here is the statement about the Xiantian Bagua (see p.32):

Heaven and Earth settle into their positions; Mountain and Marsh (or Lake) intermingle their Qi (vitality); Thunder and Wind intertwine with each other; and Water and Fire do not repel each other. The Eight Trigrams

---

8   See LieZi. *LieZi* is one of the famous philosophical books from the Warrior States (475–221 BCE) period.

interconnect with one another. To learn where we are going is the forward way. To know where we have come from is the reverse way.

In this arrangement, Qian/Heaven is located in the south, Kun/Earth is located in the north, Li/Fire is located in the east, Kan/Water is located in the west, Dui/Marsh is located in the southeast, Zhen/Thunder is located in the northeast, Xun/Wind is located in the southwest, and Gen/Mountain is located in the northwest. This arrangement stands for the great primordial cosmos before creation. It also represents a being before the birth, the prenatal time.

Let's read the next paragraph in *Shuogua* 說卦, which talks about the Houtian Bagua (see p.32):

> Supernatural Being makes everything emerge from Zhen/Thunder. All things are well arranged in Xun/Wind, meet each other in Li/Fire, obtain nourishment in Kun/Earth, celebrate in Dui/Marsh, interact in Qian/Heaven, return in Kan/Water, and achieve in Gen/Mountain.

It may be difficult for us to understand this statement. *Shuogua* 說卦 gives a further interpretation:

> Ten thousand things emerge from Zhen/Thunder. Zhen/Thunder corresponds to east. The ten thousand things are arranged well in Xun/Wind. Xun/Wind corresponds to southeast and signifies that all things are clean and neat. Li/Fire means brightness (clear), all things meet one another. It is the trigram of south. The sages face south to administer affairs of the world and govern with brightness (open heart) because of the symbolic meanings of Li/Fire. Kun is Earth, and all things absorb nourishment from Earth; therefore, it is said, "obtain nourishment in Kun." Dui/Marsh corresponds to exact autumn (west), all things rejoice; therefore, it is said, "celebrate in Dui; interact in Qian." Qian is the trigram of northwest and it represents Yin and Yang approaching each other. Kan is Water. It is the trigram of exact north and represents return (all things return); therefore, it is said, "return in Kan." Gen/Mountain is the trigram of northeast, all things achieve accomplishment and commencement; therefore, it is said, "achieve in Gen."

This arrangement represents the cosmos after creation. It also represents a person after birth or an existing object.

The Prenatal and Postnatal Bagua Arrangements are the fundamentals of the old *Yijing* divination schools. In this old divination system, no one referred to the

Yijing book because the knowledge existed long before the book was written. This divination system is based on the *Yijing* knowledge of Xiang 象 (symbolism) and Shu 數 (numerology) in the Xiantian Bagua (Prenatal Trigrams Arrangement) and Houtian Bagua (Postnatal Trigrams Arrangement).

I think we should let our brains take a rest now. Let us leave the discussion about the knowledge of Shu (numerology) and Xiang (symbolism) for the next couple of days. We should practice some Taiji Qigong again.

TAIJI QIGONG DUI 兑 (LAKE)

Let us try facing west today. The lake seems very shy in front of us. Her face is turning to pink and gold as the sun kisses her with its gentle luminosity. We should bring our eyesight back to the body. Do you remember the Qian movement we did yesterday? Please take a few minutes to review it, and then we will try the new practice of Dui.

Movement: Take a deep breath, then breathe out slowly, and gently bend your knees while you turn your right foot out to the right. In the meantime, turn your arms with right palm facing forward and left palm facing right (Figure 2). Shift your weight to your right foot and step your left foot forward while you raise your hands. Shift your weight to your left foot when your hands reach a little higher than your head (Figure 3), then bring your right foot parallel to the left foot and keep your knees slightly bent (Figure 4). Gradually straighten your legs while you drop your hands down and move back to the beginning position. Repeat this movement.

Visualization: Imagine your whole body energy sinking into the Earth, like ice melting, when you first turn your arms while bending your knees. Imagine the clouds rising when you raise your hands, and imagine the rain falling down when you drop your hands down.

Function: The shoulders and hips are your main physical spiritual gates. A good *Yijing* predictor has to relax and open the spiritual gates to connect with universal Qi during the consultation. This practice will help you release your stress and stagnation so these spiritual gates will open.

Try to sleep with your head facing west tonight. Let's meet at 11:00 a.m. tomorrow.

Figure 2

Figure 3

Figure 4

≡≡

LI 離—

DAY *3*

離為火
朋麗乎大
人以继
明照於
四方

戊子童年

Li (fire)

Zan er bu da hu shu, ze qi wei zhi wu; shu er bu da hu de, ze qi wei zhi shi... Wu yu shi wu tong tu er shu gui zhe ye.

贊而不達乎數, 則其為之巫; 數而不達乎德, 則其為之史... 吾與史巫同途而殊歸者也

If the Zan 贊 (ancient shamanic ritual with praying or chanting) does not lead to the number, then one merely acts as a shaman; if the number does not lead to virtue, then one merely acts as a scribe... I am on the same road as the scribes and shamans but end up differently.

Confucius, *Yao* 要 *(Essentials)*, from *Mawangdui Silk Book¹*

---

1   This version of the *Yijing* book was discovered in the tomb of Li Cang (d.168 BCE) at Mawangdui in Changsha, Hunan, China. It was translated into English by Edward L. Shaughnessy. See *I Ching* (New York: Ballantine Publishing Group, 1997: 241). He translated Wu 巫 as "magician." In C.G. Zhang's opinion, the best translation for Wu is "shaman." Accordingly, I use "shaman" to replace "magician." Shaughnessy translated Zan 贊 as "commendations," but I think "commendations" is not the exact meaning, so I have kept Zan.

3. Shu 數

Numerology

Yijing (*The Book of Change*) is all about the Yin-Yang principle. In fact, the whole text of the 64 hexagrams is based on two lines: the Yin line (broken line--) and the Yang line (solid line–). "One *Yin* and one *Yang* are called the Dao."[2] Ancient Chinese sages discussed the Dao in terms of Yin and Yang, determining that the union of Yin and Yang results in a state of the Dao. As we have seen in the symbolism of *Yijing*, the trigrams and hexagrams are composed of Yin lines and Yang lines that represent the Dao. Yet the interesting thing is that we can find the words Yin and Yang directly written about in the orig-

Shu (numerology)

inal Chinese version of the *Yijing* text. The Yin line is called the "six line," and the Yang line is called the "nine line."

SHUDAO 數道: THE WAY OF THE NUMBERS

Today, I am making some Red Phoenix tea for us. I pour the tea into the cups after I do the purification. We sip this dark red tea and relax in the bright sunshine.

---

2   This is from *Xici* (*Appended Statements*) of *The Book of Change*. See *I Ching* (New York: Ballantine Publishing Group, 1997: 192).

Before we start today's topic, I want to share an interesting dream I had last night. I visited the Queen Mother of the West on Kunlun Mountain. She took a scroll out of a box that was decorated with jade and pearls. She opened the scroll, and I saw a beautiful Taiji pattern made by the numbers six and nine. I remember that the six is Yin and the nine is Yang in the original *Yijing* text. This dream is a great omen for our discussion. This six and nine Yin-Yang system is related to the Five Elements numerology system, which we will discuss later. For now, it is enough to understand that the *Yijing* system originated in a numeric system.

Queen Mother of the West

Isn't it fascinating that archeological studies have determined that the symbols for the Yin and Yang lines originated from numbers?[3] Archeologists discovered that many early Gua 卦 (hexagrams or trigrams) before the Han 漢 dynasty (206 BCE–220 CE) were made with numbers, and some scholars believe that the Yin-Yang and the Five Elements theories originated in ancient numerology.[4] The *Xici* (*Appended Statements*) of *The Book of Change* states:

> The Dao of the Change proceeds by threes and fives, weaving its numbers and connecting its changes; thus, the sage completes the culture of all under Heaven, taking numbers to their limit; thus, the sage settles the images of all under Heaven.[5]

---

3   Zhou, Shan. *Zhouyi Wenhua Lun* (Shanghai: Shanghai Shehui Kexeuyuan Chubanshe, 1994: 4–10).

4   Li, Ling. *Zhongguo Fangshu Xukao* (Beijing: Dongfang Chubanshe, 2000: 96).

5   See *I Ching* (New York: Ballantine Publishing Group, 1997: 197).

Therefore, we can assume that the number system had played a main role in *Yijing* practice long before the *Yijing* book was written. Fortunately, some old *Yijing* divination knowledge is still alive in China, so I will be able to share a taste of the old divination skill with you in this book.

According to numerology theory in the *Yijing*, numbers are also categorized into Yin and Yang. Odd numbers are regarded as Yang numbers; even numbers are regarded as Yin numbers. Therefore, the Great Dao can also be represented with numbers. An ancient Chinese text on astronomy and mathematics, *Zhoubi Suanjing* 周髀算經 reputed to have been written during the Western Zhou 周 dynasty (1027–771 BCE) states, "The methods for obtaining these numbers come from the circle and the square." Renowned astronomer Zhao Shuang 趙爽 explained this in the third century CE: "The circle and square are the shapes of Heaven and Earth and embody the numbers of Yin and Yang."[6] And in the words of Liu Wansu 劉完素, a famous Jin 金 dynasty (1115–1234 CE) and Yuan 元 dynasty (1206–1368 CE) Chinese Medicine doctor, "If one gains the numbers of Heaven and Earth, one gains the great Dao."[7] As we can see, ample evidence supports the assertion that the ancient Chinese sages represented the Dao with numbers. Therefore, the function of the numbers is to access the Dao or to get answers to your questions.

Shuzhi Gua

The reason for us to learn the *Yijing* numerology is that in most *Yijing* divination systems, the key to access the answers to your questions will be Shu, the numerology. Numerology is an important foundation of *Yijing* divination. The *Yijing* divination system is called Shushu 數術 in Chinese.

---

6   Cullen, Christopher. *Astronomy and Mathematics in Ancient China* (Cambridge: Cambridge University Press, 1996: 83).

7   Wu, Jing. Wang, Yongshen. *Zhouyi Baiti Wengda: Zhouyi yu Zhongyi Oigong* (Taiyuan: Shanxi Renming Chubanshe, 1989: 38).

In Chinese, Shu 數 means number or calculation and Shu 術 means art or skill. Shushu literally means the art of numbers or calculation. Different numbers have different energetic functions, and all the divination techniques require using different numbers to carry out the calculation. Shushu includes Chinese Cosmology, Bazi Mingli 八字命理 (Principles of Your Karma or Chinese Astrology), Fengshui 風水, Baguan Yuce 八卦預測 (Eight Trigrams Divination), Liuyao Yueche 六爻預測 (Six Lines or Hexagram Divination), Qimen Dunjia 奇門遁甲 (one of the ancient Chinese prediction systems), Taiyi 太乙, and other divination systems. Are you ready for some basic knowledge of Shu, *Yijing* numerology?

HETU 河圖 AND LUOSHU 洛書: THE PATTERNS OF THE UNIVERSE

Different *Yijing* divination systems may require different numerology systems for calculation. We need to clarify which systems we will use before we begin the divination process. I have met many *Yijing* practitioners who are confused by the different *Yijing* numerology systems, even some of the well-known *Yijing* masters. As I emphasized earlier, this book will focus only on Baguan Yuce (Eight Trigrams Divination). In this divination system, we will work with two numerology systems: Xiantian Bagua Shu 先天八卦數 (Prenatal Eight Trigrams Numbers) and Tiandi Shengcheng Shu 天地生成數 (Heaven and Earth Creating and Completing Numbers). In the different stages of the Eight Trigrams Divination, we will use one of these to process the divination. Remember, these two numerology systems will be the key to access the secret answers for your questions when you play with the Baguan Yuce.

A very common *Yijing* numerology system is the Magic Square. Many Fengshui and Chinese medicine books talk about the Magic Square. In many *Yijing* divination systems, the Magic Square is very important. In Chinese, we call it Luoshu 洛書. Luoshu and another numerological pattern, Hetu 河圖, were the original source of the *Yijing*. Let's talk about Hetu and Luoshu first even though we will not use them directly in Baguan Yuce. By the way, how is your tea? Let us have another cup of tea. This Red Phoenix tea will help keep our Shen (spirit, mind) clear when we discuss these numerology systems.

Xici (*Appended Statements*) is the oldest document that refers to Hetu and Luoshu. It affirms:

Yellow River breeds Hetu and Luo River breeds Luoshu; the Sages (Enlightened Beings or *Yijing* writers) follow the way of these patterns.

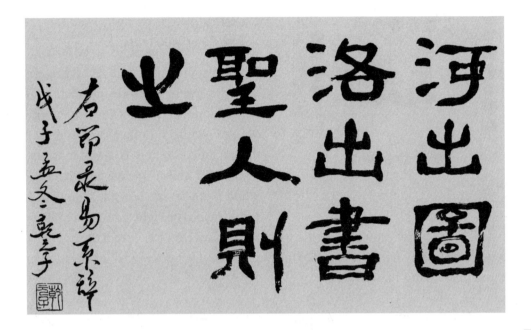

By this proclamation, we can guess that Enlightened Beings discovered the *Yijing* divination systems, trigrams, and hexagrams by studying the universal way along with Hetu and Luoshu. Some scholars have doubts about this. However, if we deepen our study, we can figure out that the Yin-Yang and Five Elements principles are a perfect fit in these two patterns. Having genuine knowledge of Hetu and Luoshu will shape your *Yijing* 易經 practice. Here, we just touch on a very superficial idea of Hetu and Luoshu.

Hetu 河圖: River Pattern

He 河 means river, and it refers specifically to the Yellow River in some Classical Chinese writing. Tu 圖 means draw, picture, image, and pattern. We can translate Hetu as "River Pattern." Actually, the original meaning of Hetu is "a pattern from the Yellow River." A Chinese myth may help us understand the origin of the name Hetu:

> In ancient times, people lived in a peaceful and harmonious environment. One day, a horse emerged from the Yellow River. Fuxi 伏羲 (the shaman king) observed the horse and noticed a special pattern on its back. He recorded the

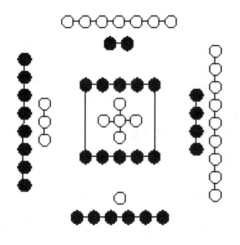

Hetu

pattern with black and white dots. People call this pattern Hetu (River Pattern) or Matu (Horse Pattern) because this pattern emerged from the Yellow River on a horse.

In this diagram, the white dots represent the Yang energy or odd numbers and the black dots represent the Yin energy or even numbers. From this, we can see that numbers 1 and 6 are at bottom, numbers 2 and 7 are on top, numbers 3 and 8 are on the left side, numbers 4 and 9 are on the right side, and numbers 5 and 10 are in the center of the diagram. Fuxi discovered the Tiandi Shengcheng Shu 天地生成數 (Heaven and Earth Creating and Completing Numbers system) through studying the Hetu.

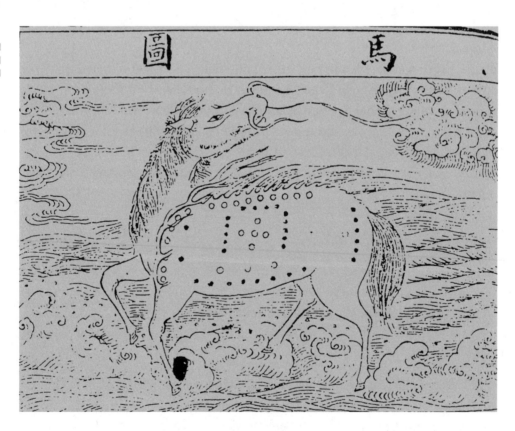

Hetu on horse

Some scholars consider this pattern to be a model of the universe.[8] According to ancient Chinese cosmology, the primordial universe was a mass of Qi. The light Qi was ascending and moving like a river, so the ancient Chinese named this flowing Qi the Tianhe 天河 (Heavenly River), and the stars emerged from the Tianhe.

Ancient shamans used numbers to express their understanding of the universe before they created Chinese characters. Ming 明 dynasty (1368–1644 CE) scholar Lai Zhide 來知德 in his book *Zhouyi Jizhu* 周易集注[9] states, "To deal with this Flowing Qi is Shu (numbers)." He drew his Taiji Hetu 太極河圖 to show his sympathetic thoughts about the Cosmos, and he expanded the numbers in the Taiji Hetu and drew an unlimited numeric pattern to represent the universal Qi. His diagram will help us understand the Heaven and Earth Creating and Completing Numbers system later.

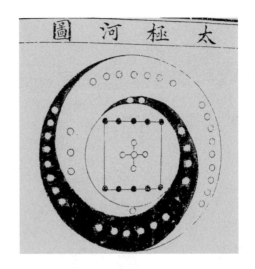

Taiji Hetu

Numeric Hetu

Luoshu 洛書: Luo Pattern

Luo 洛 means Luo River, to connect, and communication; Shu 書 means write, book, Chinese characters, calligraphy, and record. We can translate Luoshu as "Luo Pattern." Actually, the original meaning of Luoshu would be "A Pattern from Lou River." A Chinese myth may help us understand the origin of the name Luoshu:

More than 4000 years ago, there was flooding everywhere in China. Dayu 大禹 'Great Yu', the founder of the Xia 夏 dynasty (2100–1600 BCE), tried

---

8   Wang, Gongju. *Zhouyi Pangtong* (Beijing: Zgongguo Shudian, 1997: 39).

9   Lai Zhide 來知德 spent 29 years writing this book, which was published in 1602.

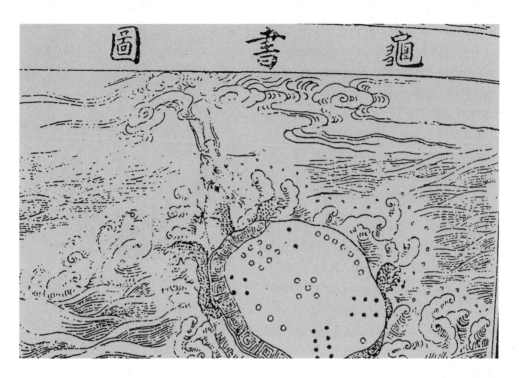

Luoshu on turtle

many different ways to stop the flood, but all of them failed. One day he stood next to the Luo River, and he saw a turtle emerging from the river. To his surprise, there was a special pattern on the back of this turtle. He observed the pattern carefully and recorded it. People call this pattern Luoshu or Guishu 龜書 (Turtle Pattern). Dayu 大禹 had a great understanding of the universal way through studying this pattern. In fact, he saved China from this great flooding by digging an elaborate system of waterways patterned after the Luoshu. Later, he became the emperor and divided China into nine states by using the Luoshu as his guide.

4	9	2
3	5	7
8	1	6

Jiugong Shu 九宮數

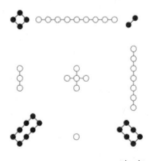

Luoshu 洛書

This story shows that Luoshu contains the universal way. You may be able to do many great things with Luoshu if you really understand the knowledge hidden within the pattern. People use this pattern in many different *Yijing* divination systems as well as in Fengshui and Chinese medicine practices.

In the Luoshu pattern, the white dots stand for the Yang numbers and the black dots stand for the Yin numbers. Let us replace the dots with numbers, and we have a new pattern made with nine numbers from one to nine. Most people know the Luoshu pattern as Jiugong Shu 九宮數, which means Nine Palaces Numbers and is commonly translated into English as Magic Square. In this pattern, no matter whether you add the three numbers on a vertical line, horizontal line, or oblique line, the sum is always 15. In Chinese tradition, the number 15 represents the harmony of life and the universe. Therefore, we consider this pattern to embody the function of the universal way or the Dao. Often, Yijing masters combine the Postnatal Eight Trigrams Arrangement with Luoshu in their consultations, and we call the new pattern Jiugong Bagua 九宮八卦 or Jiugong Bafeng 九宮八風.

Turtle and the Number 13

Let us have another cup of Red Phoenix tea, and I will share a funny number story with you. When I was on a soccer team in college, none of the other players wanted the number 13 T-shirt because they believed it was an unlucky number. This was an influence from Western culture. Then I picked the number 13 because I had a different understanding of this number and believed it was a lucky number. Everyone thought that was strange. Since east and west are opposites, the Eastern and Western cultures are also opposite. For example, you need to call 911 when you have an emergency, but in China we need to call 119. You need to call 411 for phone information, but please dial 114 if you are visiting in China. These are just some funny phenomena, so don't take them as serious cultural differences.

Over the last 30 years, archeologists have found much evidence to prove that the Jiugong Shu (Nine Palaces Numbers or the Magic Square) system existed in the divination world of the ancient Chinese shamans. In 1977, the Nine Palaces Cosmic Divination Board was excavated from an ancient tomb (165 BCE) in Shuanggudui (Double Ancient Hills), Ruyang, Anhui Province. For hundreds of years, many scholars had doubted the pre-Song 宋 dynasty (960–1279 CE)

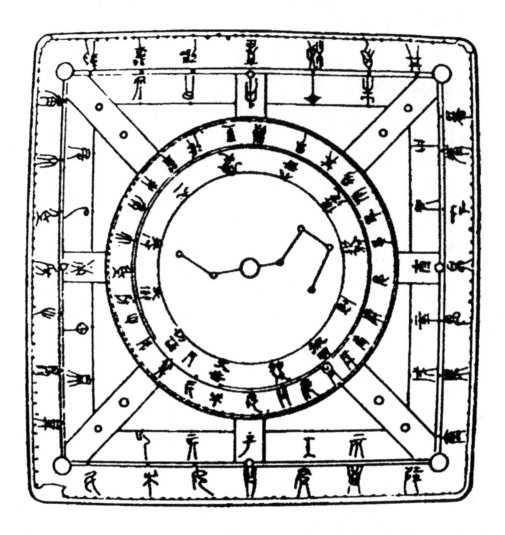

Nine Palaces Cosmic Divination Board

Jade turtle

existence of the Nine Palaces Numbers. This discovery shattered their erroneous conclusions.

A few years later, a jade turtle and a jade plaque were found on the chest of the deceased in an elaborate Neolithic burial site, which gave concrete evidence of the legend of Guishu (Turtle Pattern). This jade turtle and plaque dated to around 2500 BCE. The turtle includes a plastron and a carapace. The plastron and carapace were originally tied together through small holes on the side and the plaque was set between them. The plastron has five holes, giving us the image of the Five Elements, and the carapace has eight holes, giving us the image of the Eight Trigrams. 5 + 8 = 13. It was said that one of the original names for Taiji Quan was Thirteen because of its fundamentals of Five Elements and Eight

Jade plaque

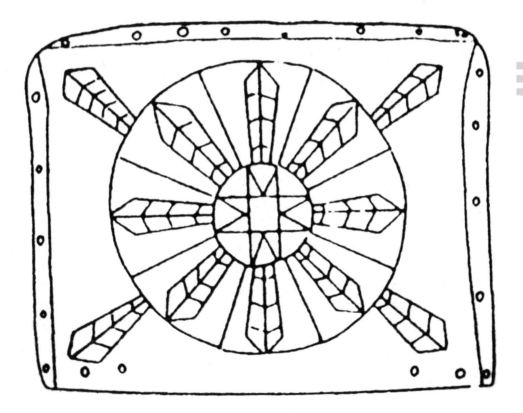

The three layers diagram engraved on the jade plaque

Trigrams. Furthermore, in traditional Chinese culture, the number 13 represents the Taibao 太保—the Great Protector. And a turtle is a symbol for armor, longevity, and divine.

The plaque is a rectangular shape that is 11 cm long and 8.2 cm wide.[10] Each wide side has five holes, one long side has nine holes, and the other long side has four holes. Double rows of five holes give us the feeling of stability. The nine holes and four holes give us another pattern of the number 13 and the image of Heaven (nine) and Earth (four). A diagram was engraved on this plaque, and it gives us more images. The diagram has three layers. In the central layer, we can see an octagon connecting with the four directions. In the middle layer, we can see eight arrows pointing to the eight directions. And in the outer layer, we can see four arrows pointing to the four corner directions. Many scholars think this plaque was the legend of Guishu (Turtle Pattern or Turtle Book). You might find all the knowledge of Yin and Yang, Wuxing (Five Elements), Hetu, Luoshu, Jiugong, and Bagua hidden within this jade plaque.

TIANDI SHENGCHENG SHU 天地生成數: HEAVEN AND EARTH CREATING AND COMPLETING NUMBERS

Tiandi Shengcheng Shu, the Heaven and Earth Creating and Completing Numbers system, is related to the description in *Xici* (*Appended Statements*):

> Heaven One, Earth Two, Heaven Three, Earth Four, Heaven Five, Earth Six, Heaven Seven, Earth Eight, Heaven Nine, Earth Ten.

Other *Yijing* divination texts give us more details about this system:

> Heaven One generates Water; Earth Six accomplishes it. Earth Two generates Fire; Heaven Seven accomplishes it. Heaven Three generates Wood; Earth Eight accomplishes it. Earth Four generates Metal; Heaven Nine accomplishes it. Heaven Five generates Earth; Earth Ten accomplishes it.

Let us draw a map for this description according to the Five Elements principle:

---

10 Feng, Shi. *Archaeoastronomy in China* (Beijing: Zhongguo Shehui Kexue Chubanshe, 2007: 503).

2 **South** 7

Fire

3 **East** 8   5 **Center** 10   4 **West** 9

Wood   Earth   Metal

1 **North** 6

Water

We can see that this map is equal to the Hetu if we convert the dots to numbers. We can clearly see that the numbers one and six are equal to the Water element and are located in the north. Two and seven are equal to the Fire element and are located in the south. Three and eight are equal to the Wood element and are located in the east. Four and nine are equal to the Metal element and are located in the west. Five and ten are equal to the Earth element and are located in the center.

The five numbers 1, 2, 3, 4, and 5 are called the Five Elements Creating Numbers and 6, 7, 8, 9, and 10 are called the Five Elements Completing Numbers. The scholar Lai Zhide gave us some valuable information about these numbers when he explained his Taiji Hetu in *Zhouyi Jizhu*:

> Although the Five Creating Numbers control the Five Completing Numbers, all of the Creating Numbers stay in the inner layer and all of the Completing Numbers stay in the outer layer. Both Yin and Yang energies move from the inner layer to the outer layer. The result is that both the odd Yang numbers (1, 3, 5, 7, and 9) and the Yin numbers (2, 4, 6, and 8) move in sequence from smaller to larger.

From Lai Zhide's Taiji Hetu, we can tell that these Yin and Yang numbers are moving together like a spiral, and this shows the way of creation or the birth of new life.

THE RELATIONSHIPS AMONG NUMEROLOGY, YIN-YANG, AND FIVE ELEMENTS

In the numerology of the *Yijing*, 1, 2, 3, 4, and 5 are the Creation or Foundation Numbers. All of the other numbers emerge from these five numbers. These five numbers also contain the theory of Yin and Yang and the principle of the Five Elements. Heaven belongs to Yang and Earth belongs to Yin. The Yang numbers (1, 3, and 5) are Heavenly numbers, and the Yin numbers (2 and 4) are Earthly numbers. The *Shuogua* commentary discusses the "Heavenly three and Earthly two." The *Yizhiyi* 易之義 (*Properties of the Change*) commentary in the *Mawangdui Yijing* 馬王堆易經 manuscript describes "Joining with the Three of Heaven and the Two of Earth and so giving birth to all of the numbers."[11]

As we discussed in the beginning of this chapter, in *The Book of Change*, the Yang line in the hexagrams is represented by the number nine while the Yin line is represented by the number six. We have been wondering why the lines use nine and six to replace the characters Yin and Yang to express the Dao. The answer is hidden in the Five Elements Creating Numbers: "the Three of Heaven and the Two of Earth." $1 + 3 + 5 = 9$. Nine is the highest Yang number produced directly from the three Heavenly Creation Numbers. As the purest Yang number, nine manifests Heaven. $2 + 4 = 6$. Six is the highest Yin number produced directly from the two Earthly Foundation Numbers. As the purest Yin number, six manifests Earth. Therefore, nine represents the Yang energy and six represents the Yin energy.

I think the concept of Yin and Yang emerged along with the numerology. In ancient China before the Chinese characters were invented, Wu (shamans) had been practicing divination by numerology for a long time. Of course, I presume they applied the concept and principle of Yin and Yang in their divination. After many generations, they invented the Chinese characters and wrote down their experiential knowledge. The *Yijing* (*The Book of Change*) is one of these early texts. Although we are not able to find single words of Yin and Yang in the original text, we can tell that the *Yijing* contains the principle of Yin and Yang. The numbers six and nine in the text indicate that the Wu (shamans) finished the original text of *Yijing* before they invented the Chinese characters for Yin and Yang.

I sip the tea and reflect on the relationship between the Five Elements

---

11 The *Mawangdui Yijing* 馬王堆易經 was discovered in the tomb of Li Cang (approximately 168 BCE) at Mawangdui in Changsha, Hunan, China.

philosophy and *Yijing*. Is there any information about the Five Elements in the original text? In fact, I haven't seen any information about the Five Elements in the original *Yijing* text. Actually, the text that gives birth to the concept of the Five Elements and clarifies how the five numbers are related to the Five Elements is the *Hongfan* 洪范 (Great Model). It is one of the oldest of the ancient Chinese classics and is thought to have been written early in the Western Zhou dynasty (1027–771 BCE). This text specifies, "One is Water, two is Fire, three is Wood, four is Metal, and five is Earth."[12]

The *Hongfan* text also discusses the idea that the universe is composed of the Five Elements and that the universal way (Great Dao) can be expressed by the Five Elements. The Five Elements create a bridge of relationship between human beings and the universe. Through this relationship, we are able to understand how human beings communicate with the universe. Therefore, the Heaven and Earth Creating and Completing Numbers system holds the foundation of the Five Elements.

Have another cup of tea, please. Try to remember the relationship between the ten numbers and Five Elements if you can because we need to apply this knowledge in our future divination or healing practice.

XIANTIAN BAGUA SHU 先天八卦數: PRENATAL EIGHT TRIGRAMS NUMBERS

We will use the Xiantian Bagua Shu (Prenatal Eight Trigrams Numbers) in an early stage of the divination. With this system, we will be able to decode the trigram that is related to our questions during the divination in Baguan Yuce (Eight Trigrams Divination).

From the name, you may infer that this system originated from the Xiantian Bagua (Prenatal Trigrams Arrangement). In this arrangement, Qian/Heaven is located in the south, Kun/Earth is located in the north, Li/Fire is located in the east, Kan/Water is located in the west, Dui/Marsh is located in the southeast, Gen/Mountain is located in the northwest, Zhen/Thunder is located in the northeast, and Xun/Wind is located in the southwest. Each trigram is associated with a number: Qian is one, Kun is eight, Li is three, Kan is six, Dui is two, Gen is seven, Zhen is four, and Xun is five. In this numerology system, one is equal to

---

12   See *Baihua Shangshu* (Xian: Sanqin Chubanshe, 1998: 98).

the trigram Qian, two is equal to the trigram Dui, three is equal to the trigram Li, four is equal to the trigram Zhen, five is equal to the trigram Xun, six is equal to the trigram Kan, seven is equal to the trigram Gen, and eight is equal to the trigram Kun. These eight numbers form a dynamic Taiji pattern in the Prenatal Trigrams Arrangement which represents the creation of life or the universe.

You may want to know why these eight numbers are related to the Eight Trigrams in such a way. The answer is in a description from the *Xici* (*Appended Statements*):

> Therefore, the Yi has the Taiji, and it gives birth to the Liangyi; the Liangyi gives birth to the Sixiang; and the Sixiang gives birth to the Bagua.

This description shows the creating process of life or the universe. It makes sense to me that the Yi (changes or transformations) is about life because modern science

Taiji pattern in the Prenatal Trigrams Arrangement

has mapped cell division in its progression from one cell to two cells to four cells to eight cells.

Let us look at the Bagua birth diagram below. It will help you understand the details of why these eight numbers are in this order.

This is the diagram of Yi 易 (changes or transformations). Please start at the bottom and move up to the top layer of this diagram. The bottom layer ☯ is the symbol of Taiji 太極, which represents the universal life force. This life force creates two components of life energy, Yin (--) and Yang (–), known as the Liangyi 兩儀, and shown on the second layer. It represents two expressions of the opposing universal energy, Heaven and Earth. Just as in human cell division, each component generates two new components. The Yin (--) generates Taiyin 太陰 (Great Yin), which is composed of two broken Yin lines, and Shaoyang 少陽 (Lesser Yang), which is composed of one Yin line on the bottom and one Yang line on the top. The Yang (–) generates Shaoyin 少陰 (Lesser Yin), which is composed of one Yang line on the bottom and one Yin line on the top, and Taiyang 太陽 (Great Yang), which is composed of two Yang lines. These four new components are Sixiang 四象, as shown on the third layer of the diagram. It represents the four spiritual animals in the sky: Qinglong 青龍, Green Dragon in the east; Baihu 白虎, White Tiger in the west; Zhuque 朱雀, Red Bird in the south; and Xuanwu 玄武, Black Warrior in the north. It is also symbolic of time and refers to the four seasons of the year. In the same fashion as the division of components,

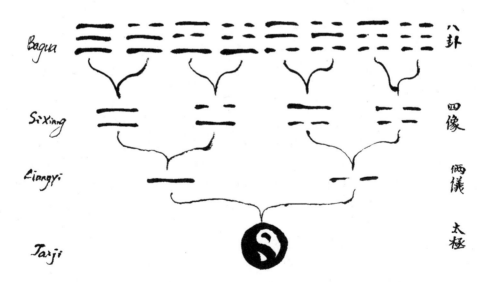

Bagua birth diagram

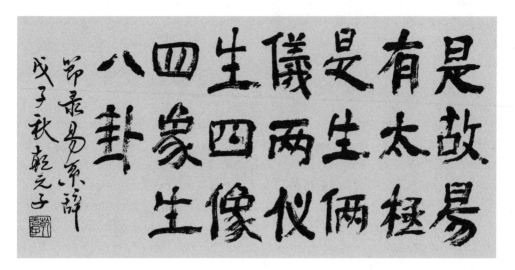

The Yi has the Taiji, and it gives birth to the Liangyi; the Liangyi gives birth to the Sixiang; and the Sixiang gives birth to the Bagua

the Sixiang 四象 produces the Eight Trigrams, Bagua 八卦, as they are shown on the top layer. Taiyin (Great Yin) produces Kun 坤 (Earth) and Gen 艮 (Mountain); Shaoyang (Lesser Yang) produces Kan 坎 (Water) and Xun 巽 (Wind); Shaoyin (Lesser Yin) produces Zhen 震 (Thunder) and Li 離 (Fire); Taiyang (Great Yang) produces Dui 兌 (Lake) and Qian 乾 (Heaven).

I hope that you are clear about the relationship between the eight numbers and the Eight Trigrams now. The order of the eight numbers is the order of the Eight Trigrams from left to right on the top layer of the diagram. This order embodies the information of the creation of a new life or the universe. Each number in these Prenatal Eight Trigrams Numbers stands for the corresponding trigram, and it is the key to open the storehouse of answers when you do the Eight Trigrams divination.

In general, we use the Prenatal Eight Trigrams Numbers in the early stage of the divination. We use Tiandi Shengcheng Shu, the Heaven and Earth Creating and Completing Numbers system, in the late stage of the divination. It will help us find a way to fix a problem. Healers can find a better prescription or more effective healing work for their clients if they master this numerology system.

TAIJI QIGONG LI 離 (FIRE)

It is time for us to try a new movement in our practice. The light is so bright outside on this sunny late afternoon. We walk south of the tea house and I feel the fragrance of the flowers sinking into my heart. Let us just relax here and soak in the light and warmth for a few minutes. Now we can review the Taiji Qigong Qian and Dui then start the new practice of Li.

Movement: Shift your weight to your right foot and step your left foot forward. In the meantime, swing your fingers to your center front, bringing your left middle finger to the same level as the tip of your nose and your right hand to the same level as your left elbow (Figure 5). Then turn your torso 45 degrees to the right and keep your head upright and facing forward (Figure 6). Next, turn your torso 45 degrees back and shift your weight to your left leg; then bring your right foot parallel to the left foot, keeping your knees slightly bent with palms facing each other, shoulder-width apart (Figure 7). Gradually straighten your legs while you turn your hands forward (Figure 8). Drop your hands down to the front of your lower belly with your right hand making a fist facing your belly (Figure 9).

Visualization: Feel your whole body full of Qi, or light. When you swing your fingers, imagine yourself like the axis of a wheel when you turn your torso. Imagine

Figure 5

Figure 6

93

Figure 7

Figure 8

Figure 9

you are putting the universal Qi into your belly when your right hand makes the fist.

Function: The heart is the emperor of the body, and the body is your nation. A great emperor will lead a great nation. This practice will help you strengthen your heart function and find the power of your spirituality. Therefore, this practice will bring you into a healthy and harmonious state. In this state, the result of your *Yijing* consulting should be very close to the truth.

Now you can enjoy the nice sunshine, birds, and Nature on your own. I want you to get up earlier tomorrow morning. I hope 6:00 a.m. will work for you. You can stay in the guest room on the south side of the tea house tonight. I hope you will have a sweet dream.

ZHEN 震一
DAY 4

Zhen (thunder)

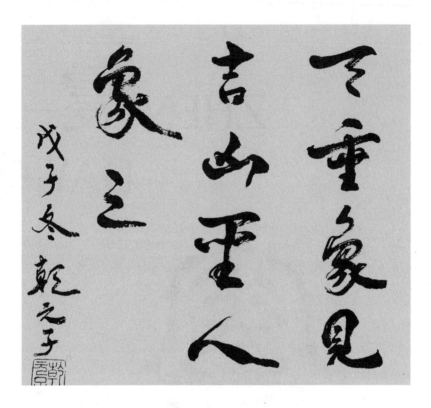

Tian chui xiang xian ji xiong, sheng ren xiang zhi.

天垂象, 見吉凶, 聖人象之.[1]

Heaven showed its pattern; it indicated auspicious and inauspicious, and the Sage made a symbol of it.

---

1 *Yijing. Xici (Appended Statements).* See *Zhouyi Shangshixue* (Beijing: Zhonghua Shuju, 1988: 301).

4. Xiang 象

Symbolism

The *Yijing* divination system was developed before Chinese characters were invented. The original *Yijing* text was composed of only Gua 卦 (trigrams or hexagrams) and had no written language. One had to master the symbolic meanings of Gua 卦 to do a good job in the *Yijing* prediction or divination. The *Xici* (*Appended Statements*) states: "Yi zhe 易者, Xiang ye 象也." This means Yi (change or prediction) is all about Xiang (symbol). A good *Yijing* predictor would never depend on the written *Yijing* text. Therefore, we have to discuss the symbolic meanings, Xiang, of the Bagua (Eight Trigrams) before we talk about how to do *Yijing* prediction.

Xiang (symbol)

XIANG 象: SYMBOLISM

Bagua chenglie, xiang zai qi zhong.

八卦成列, 象在其中矣.

Eight Trigrams complete their arrangement; symbols are within it.[2]

---

2   See *Yijing. Xici (Appended Statements).*

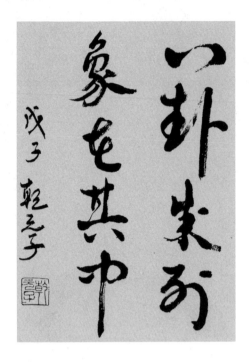

I am preparing the pure Longjing (Dragon Well) tea for our early morning meeting. This is one of the best-quality green teas in the world, and it grows in my home province of Zhejiang in eastern China. I visited my hometown a few months ago and brought it back with me.

I take a small sip of my tea and take a look at the view through the window on the east side of the tea house. It is not as strong as the tea we have been drinking the last couple of days, but I do like the subtle flavor of this tea. It makes me feel very calm.

The dawn is breaking through the darkness. The gold, red, pink, yellow, white, and black clouds look like they're painted on the deep-blue eastern sky. The thick white cloud below is covering the cedars. It looks like an ocean. After a few minutes, the sun jumps out from the cloud ocean. Suddenly, the whole eastern sky opens its new face with shining golden light. Let us bring this image back to the Dantian and meditate with it for a few minutes. This eastern new-life energy will support today's discussion.

The most basic *Yijing* divination technique is observation. Once we observe an object, we obtain an image or a picture of it. We call this image or picture Xiang in Chinese. The original meaning of Xiang is elephant. The elephant is the largest land animal in the world and can easily be recognized by its physical features. Elephants were numerous in the central area of ancient China; in fact, the oldest Chinese character for elephant looks like a picture of an elephant. A natural phenomenon is as easy to recognize as the shape of an elephant.[3]

Xiang is similar to English word symbols according to philosopher Susanne Langer's definition:

A symbol is any **thing** which may function as the vehicle for a conception.

---

3   Wu, Zhongxian. *Vital Breath of the Dao: Chinese Shamanic Tiger Qigong* (St Paul, MN: Dragon Door Publications, 2006: 43).

Such a thing may be a word, a mathematical notation, an act, a gesture, a ritual, a dream, a work of art, or anything else that can carry a concept. The concept may be a rational-linguistic one, an imagined-intuitive one, or a feeling-evaluative one. It makes no difference as long as the symbol carries it effectively. The concept is the symbol's meaning.[4]

Ancient Chinese shamans used Xiang (symbols) as vehicles to access different universal energies for healing and divination. It will be easy to master the *Yijing* divination techniques if we master the Guaxiang 卦象, the symbolic meanings of a Gua (trigram). Each Gua has many different symbolic meanings, and these symbolic meanings are the answers to our questions when we do a divination. We will not be able to decode our answers from a Gua if we do not know the symbolic meanings.

Let us sit next to the tea tray again to have another cup of tea. Please take a careful look at this picture.

Two sets of tea cups

---

4   This theory of symbolism is from Susanne Langer's *Philosophy in a New Key* (Cambridge, MA: Harvard University Press, 1942). Additional analysis comes from Donald Sander in *Navaho Symbols of Healing* (Rochester, VT: Healing Arts Press, 1991).

What do you notice? Yes, two Gongfu tea sets are filled with tea. If I ask you how many people you think were drinking tea together when I took this picture, it would be easy for you to tell if you know something about Gongfu tea. However, if you show this picture to people who have never had any experience with Gongfu tea, can they tell what is going on in the picture? The symbolic meanings of a trigram are just like this picture; the image is very clear to everyone who has knowledge beyond the surface of the image. We can decode a correct answer from a trigram if we understand its symbolic meanings and its energetic relationship to our question.

We have to be careful because we may feel very frustrated when we first learn the symbolic meanings of a trigram if we are without patience. Let us take a sip of this new Longjing tea and enjoy a piece of Chinese poetry before we learn the Guaxiang 卦象.

Xiaoqiao, liushui, renjia

小橋，流水，人家

"Little bridge, flowing water, and family"

This piece of poetry is very simple but is quite well known in China. These few simple words create an abstract Daoist landscape. We have to use our hearts to meditate on this harmonious landscape through these words. Without a heartfelt connection, this piece of poetry is just a few words to us.

The way of study with *Yijing* is like the way of appreciating a classical Chinese poem. Many layers of the symbolic meanings might be only chaotic words to us if we just interpret the words at the literal meaning. We need to slow down, in the same way we savor the tea, to feel the energetic connection through different words. The new cup of tea is ready. Please take three sips and look out the windows again.

Can you tell me anything about the special features of this Celestial Tea House? This octagonal building is related to an Eight Trigrams Arrangement. It follows the pattern of the Postnatal Eight Trigrams Arrangement. Each side of the building is related to one of the trigrams. Would you like to discuss some symbolic meanings of each trigram through each side of this Celestial Tea House with me?

GUAXIANG 卦象: THE SYMBOLIC MEANING OF THE BAGUA 八卦

As we discussed a couple of days ago, *Yijing* has two arrangements of the Bagua: the Prenatal Eight Trigrams and the Postnatal Eight Trigrams. Each of these two arrangements has the same Eight Trigrams but in a different order. Now let us ignore the order and focus on the Guaxiang, the symbolic meaning of each single Gua (trigram). Each trigram in a different situation has a different symbolic meaning.

☰ Qian 乾 Heaven, Sky

Please take a look at the view from the northwest side of the tea house. What image do you get? Yes, the clear and transparent blue sky. In *Yijing*, we use three unbroken lines to represent this image of sky, and this is the trigram of Qian. The original meaning of Qian is the rising Qi or energy. The ascending Qi formed Heaven, according to ancient Chinese cosmology, so the trigram Qian represents Heaven. By Heaven we mean not just Heaven or sky but the functions of the universe—movements of the planets and stars. The movement of cosmos is absolutely there, and this is the energetic meaning of Qian. The three unbroken lines

of Qian are the image of the quality of the sky. We could use the trigram Qian to represent anything that has the quality of the rising up spirit or the sky in the energetic level.

As we look at the sky with the heart, we may feel the majestic power of the universe. It is so deep and gives us a great and penetrating feeling. It looks like a hemispheric lid—and the sun, moon, and stars never stop their running. This gives us a feeling of strength as well as a round shape, circular. So, some symbolic meanings of the trigram Qian are strong, circular, round, penetrating, great, and spin. Actually, in the early Han dynasty (206 BCE–220 CE) *Mawangdui Silk Book* version of the *Yijing*,[5] the name for this trigram with three unbroken lines was written as Jian 鍵, which means strong. The radical on the right side of the character Jian is related to the Big Dipper. The Big Dipper is the universal clock that never stops running; its handle shows the way.

---

5   The *Mawangdui Yijing* manuscript was discovered in the tomb of Li Cang (d. 168 BCE) at Mawangdui, in Changsha, Hunan, China in 1973.

Qian represents Jīn 金 (Metal element) if we talk about its features from the perspective of the Five Elements principle. The quality of Metal is clear, penetrating, sharp, strong, immortal, sensitive, and transparent. And Qian represents cold weather if we want to get a weather prediction. I'll list some symbolic meanings of Qian as a reference for our future divination.

Element: Metal

Weather: snow, hail, ice, frost, cold

Location: capital, big city, high place

Person: president, father, old man, senior generation, government official, famous person, wise man

Personality: strong, brave, sharp, straight, active, sensitive

Body: head, bones, lung, large intestines

Time: autumn, 7:00–9:00 p.m., Metal element of the year, month, day

Animal: horse (stallion), swan, lion, elephant

Small, still object: gold, jade, jewelry, round-shaped object, round fruit, hard object, hat, mirror

Building: house located in the northwest, mansion, government hall, tall building

Direction: northwest in Postnatal Trigrams Arrangement, south in Prenatal Trigrams Arrangement

Number: 1, 4, 9

Flavor: pungent, spicy

Color: deep red, white

☱ Dui 兌 Marsh, Lake

Now let us take a look at the view from the west side of the tea house. At the foot of the hill, the lake looks like a shy young woman who is covering her face with the mist scarf. Her face starts to shine when she secretly smiles at the sun. After a while, she takes off the scarf, and we can see her magical face.

Ancient Chinese shamans considered a lake or marsh to be an open mouth of the Earth that they could communicate with to learn the answers to their questions. You might be able to tell what the environmental situation is in your area if you understand the changes that have happened in a lake or marsh in the area. We use the trigram Dui with one broken line on top and two solid lines at the bottom to represent this energetic quality of Dui.

The original meaning of the Chinese character Dui is speak. We have to open the mouth when we speak, so mouth is one of the symbolic meanings of the trigram Dui. It also means the ability to negotiate and communicate. The mouth relates to an open, broken quality. Like Qian, it has a Metal quality but has more to do with the communication part of Metal: sharp, broken, and opening. Here is the list of some symbolic meanings of Dui:

Element: Metal

Weather: rain shower, star, new moon

Location: marsh, ruined pond or well

Person: young woman, concubine, actress, interpreter, shaman

Personality: joyful, happy, talkative

Body: mouth, lung, saliva, joints

Time: autumn, 3:00–5:00 p.m., Metal element of the year, month, and day

Animal: goat, sheep

Small, still object: knife, metal tools or equipment, broken thing

Building: house located in the west or near a marsh

Direction: west in Postnatal Trigrams Arrangement, southeast in Prenatal Trigrams Arrangement

Number: 2, 4, 9

Flavor: pungent, spicy

Color: white

☲ Li 離 Fire

On the south side of the tea house, colorful flowers are lifting their heads and washing their faces with the dew. Somehow, I always have a feeling of great excitement when I look at red flowers in the early morning. I feel they really wake up my Shen (spirit). The feeling might be similar to the feeling some people have when they drink a cup of delicious coffee first thing in the morning. Also, birds seem to like early morning life. They are singing their favorite songs while looking for their breakfast. Let us move our eyesight farther along to where the sky is painted with many different patterns of red clouds. We can use the trigram Li with one Yin line between two Yang lines to represent this sight.

The original meaning of the Chinese character Li is the name for a bird with colorful feathers. It stands for colorful and bright. In Chinese shamanic traditions, a bird represents the spirit, and it is the spiritual animal of the Heart. In the *Mawangdui Yijing* manuscript, the trigram Li is written as Luo 罗 and means net.

The image of the trigram Li, with the inside broken and the outside solid, shows another symbolic meaning: softness hidden within and hardness expressed outward. Fire has this same quality because the outer layers of the flame have a much higher temperature than the inner layers. The outside is strong and the inside is gentle. The trigram Li is also a symbol for fire. It manifests heart, Shen (spirit), mind, emperor, wisdom, eyes, hot, advance, light, sun, and brightness. Here is the list of some symbolic meanings of Li:

Element: Fire

Weather: sunny, lightning, rainbow

Location: dry location, southern place, fireplace, stove

Person: middle-aged woman, scholar, big-bellied person, armed person

Personality: humble, intelligent

Body: eyes, heart, small intestines

Time: summer, 11:00 a.m.–1:00 p.m., Fire element of the year, month, and day

Animal: pheasant, turtle, shellfish, crab

Small, still object: light, bright object, window, net

Building: house located in the south, bright house

Direction: south in Postnatal Trigrams Arrangement, east in Prenatal Trigrams Arrangement

Number: 3, 2, 7

Flavor: bitter

Color: red, violet

☳ Zhen 震 Thunder

We look at the view from the east side of the tea house again. The landscape seems changed from ten minutes ago. The thick cloud ocean is no longer there. We can see some of the mist still wandering among the cedar trees. The sunlight is penetrating through the mist to wake up all the life in this cedar forest. This scenery is one of the symbolic patterns of the trigram Zhen, which has one solid line at the bottom and two broken lines on top. The shape looks like a bowl with the top open and a stable, solid bottom.

The Chinese character Zhen means shake, vibration, or move. Thunder represents this quality of shaking, the vibration of the world shaking. From the

perspective of ancient Chinese shamanism, the roaring of thunder is the spirit of Nature that wakes up all beings and creates more new-life energy. In modern China, we often still use the words ChunLei 春雷 (spring thunder) to represent the coming of new life.

In China, the thunder season happens in springtime, and you can hear much more thunder in the east part of China. Therefore, this trigram represents the spring season, and it belongs to the Wood element in the Five Elements principle:

Element:	Wood
Weather:	thunder
Location:	forest, noisy place, big road, bamboo grove
Person:	older man, first son in a family
Personality:	angry, shocking, loud, hyperactive, compassionate
Body:	foot, liver, fingernails, toenails, voice, gallbladder
Time:	spring, 5:00–7:00 a.m., Wood element of the year, month, and day
Animal:	dragon, snake
Small, still object:	wood or bamboo object, musical instrument, flowers
Building:	house located in the east or in a forest, gazebo
Direction:	east in Postnatal Trigrams Arrangement, northeast in Prenatal Trigrams Arrangement
Number:	4, 8, 3
Flavor:	sour
Color:	green

☴ Xun 巽 Wind

When we look at the view from the southeast side of the tea house, the bamboo garden enters into our eyes. The green color of the bamboo looks very fresh in this early morning, and it seems like green jade liquid flowing down to the ground through the bamboo trunks. The calming breeze slowly makes the leaves

shake. We can use the trigram Xun, which has one broken line at the bottom and two solid lines on the top, to represent this view. This image of wind blowing bamboo shows us the energetic meaning of the trigram Xun showing off its strength and its inner flexibility. Xun is a symbol for vitality and life energy, and it has strong momentum.

The Chinese character Xun means magnificent or prepared, and it is the symbol for Wind. Wind belongs to the Wood element. The attribute of Wind is the ability to proceed and to propagate gently. It manifests Qi, breath, romantic love, news, order, and discipline. Ancient shamans understand that both Wind and Wood energy originated in the east. In the realm of Heaven, the presence of spirit expresses and manifests itself in the form of Wind. In the Earth, spirit expresses itself in the lushness and aliveness of "wood" (plants). The virtue of Wood is to gently push and advance the expansion of harmonious Qi. Here is the list for some symbolic meanings of the trigram Xun:

Element: Wood

Weather: windy

Location: garden, southeastern place

Person:	older woman, widow, monk
Personality:	sweet, hesitant, artistic
Body:	thigh, meridians
Time:	transition between spring and summer, 7:00–9:00 a.m.
Animal:	rooster, chicken, hen, birds
Small, still object:	string, long and straight thing, artwork
Building:	house located in the southeast or in a forest, temple
Direction:	southeast in Postnatal Trigrams Arrangement, southwest in Prenatal Trigrams Arrangement
Number:	5, 8, 3
Flavor:	sour
Color:	green

 ☵ Kan 坎 Water

We look at the view from the north side of the tea house. We can see the "Golden Mountain" because the color of the snow on the mountain turns to a beautiful, glistening golden color during this sunrise period. This image shows part of the mystical quality of the cold-water element because the water (snow) is showing off some of its hidden qualities at this moment. We might never have had a chance to see this gorgeous view if we hadn't gotten up early. We can use the trigram Kan, which has one unbroken line between two broken lines, to represent this view.

The Chinese character Kan means entrapment, trap, danger, collapse, or difficult. The trigram Kan shows us the hardness or strong power hidden under the surface of weakness or softness. Water is the presenter of this trigram. Water contains a dangerous quality, like a hidden trap. For example, deep water, rivers, lakes, and oceans may look peaceful and quiet on the surface, but this can be deceiving. That is the mystical part of water, the unknown. Chinese shamans believe that Water is the most mystical element because it came first from Heaven, and all life began in water. We still use water as the most important medicine in our healing process.

In the *Mawangdui Yijing* manuscript, this Kan trigram is listed as Gan 贛, which means to bestow. The trigram Kan is the symbol for water and represents Kidney, Jing (essence) in the body. Its meanings include cold, softness, moist, surrender, flowing, intelligence, darkness, mystery, benefit, moon, and virtue. Here is the list of some symbolic meanings of Kan:

Element: Water

Weather: rainy, moon, snow, frost, dew

Location: river, lake, spring, well, northern place, wetland

Person: middle-aged man, fisherman, thief, artist

Personality: flexible, flowing, wise

Body: ears, blood, kidneys

Time: winter, 11:00 p.m.–1:00 a.m., Water element of the year, month, and day

Animal: pig, fish

Small, still object: nuts, bow, wheel, bottle, wine cup

Building: house located in the north or near water

Direction: north in Postnatal Trigrams Arrangement, west in Prenatal Trigrams Arrangement

Number: 1, 6

Flavor: salty

Color: black

☶ Gen 艮 Mountain

We look at the view from the northeast side of the tea house and see that the long-stretching mountain ridge is holding the edge of the sky. A long, narrow

strand of clouds looks like a free dragon slowly moving at the waist of the mountain. This image gives me the feeling of stability and mystical transformation. We can use the trigram Gen, which has one unbroken line on top and two broken lines at the bottom. This trigram looks like an overturned bowl and gives us a very stable feeling.

The Chinese character Gen means stop, hold, or stability. A mountain represents the stability and spiritual quality of the trigram Gen. Cultivation has to do with the mountain—seeking stability. Hermits and monks are always related to the mountain because they find stability internally, like the mountain. Actually, the Chinese character Xian 仙 for immortal is simply made up of an image of a person (the left radical Ren 人) next to a mountain (the right radical Shan 山). Chinese shamans see the back as the mountain of the body. We should always straighten the back to support our life energy and maintain stability. This is a simple way to strengthen our physical body, mind, and spirit. By doing this, we are constantly bringing our minds back to our bodies. The inability to sit calmly shows an inability of the mind to maintain stability.

The trigram Gen belongs to the Earth element because of the stability of Earth. It represents the hand, back, and stomach in the body. On the negative side, it represents stagnation energy. Here is the list of some symbolic meanings of the trigram Gen:

Element: Earth

Weather: cloudy, fog

Location: mountain, hiking trail, tomb

Person: young man, mountain person

Personality: quiet, slow, stable, hidden, stubborn

Body: hand, bones, nose, back, spleen, stomach

Time: between winter and summer, 1:00–3:00 a.m., Earth element of the year, month, and day

Animal: dog, tiger, rat

Small, still object: pebbles, fruit, peanut

Building: house located in the northeast or near a rock or trail

Direction: northeast in Postnatal Trigrams Arrangement, northwest in Prenatal Trigrams Arrangement

Number: 5, 7, 10

Flavor: sweet

Color: yellow, brown

☷ Kun 坤 Earth

Now let us take a look at the view from the southwest side of the tea house. This is rich farmland, and we have fresh organic fruits and vegetables all year round from the local farmers here. I love the delicious local cheese. Now, cows and oxen are relaxing on the land. They seem to be enjoying this peaceful, quiet morning. Some of them are sluggish after eating their breakfast, and some are taking a morning nap. The trigram Kun, which has three broken lines, represents the Earth quality of openness, greatness, carrying everything. Like the mother, the Earth holds everything.

The Chinese character Kun 坤 is made by the left radical Tu 土, which means Earth element, and the right radical Shen 申, which means stretch, lightning, or

spirit. Kun stands for the Nature spirits that are hidden within the Earth. Earth does not show off, yet it holds, carries, and supports all beings. In shamanic inner cultivation, we believe that the upper Dantian is the Heaven of the body, the middle Dantian is the human being of the body, and the lower Dantian is the Earth of the body. We always need to ground and connect to the lower Dantian because the Earth holds the spirit. Here is the list of some symbolic meanings of Kun:

Element: Earth

Weather: cloudy, foggy

Location: field, countryside, flat place

Person: mother, old woman, farmer, peasant, many people, big-bellied person

Personality: gentle, soft, cowardly

Body: belly, spleen, stomach, flesh

Time: 1:00–3:00 p.m., Earth element of the year, month, and day

Animal: cow, ox, horse (mare)

Small, still object: silk, corner-shaped thing, grain, car, pottery

Building: house located in the southwest, storage unit, short building, building made of adobe

Direction: southwest in Postnatal Trigrams Arrangement, north in Prenatal Trigrams Arrangement

Number: 8, 5, 10

Flavor: sweet

Color: yellow, brown, black

This information on the symbolic meanings of each trigram may seem to be chaotic and hard to understand at first. We will discuss some energetic connections of the symbolic meanings tomorrow when we start playing with the prediction or divination. However, you still need to remember these meanings if you want to be skilled at playing with the *Yijing* divination because this information will help you figure out the inner connection between your questions and answers during your future prediction practice. You will understand all of the meanings if you keep playing with them in the future. Besides, the most important foundation for *Yijing* prediction is Shenming 神明, which means spiritual brightness or Enlightenment. We will be able to understand the symbolic meanings of the trigrams and easily find the answer during the *Yijing* consultation if we continue our inner cultivation. Now let us leave the trigrams and start our Taiji Qigong practice.

Shenming (spiritual brightness or enlightenment)

TAIJI QIGONG ZHEN 震 (THUNDER)

Now we can see the cedars clearly because the clouds that were on top of them are gone. Through the sunlight, we can see a very gentle belt of mist that looks like a mystical dragon arising from the trees. I take a deep breath, bring my eyesight back to my body, and feel my body connect with that mystical dragon. After repeating the practice of Taiji Qigong Qian, Dui, and Li several times, we start our new practice of Zhen for today.

Movement: Please check your posture after the Li practice. Make sure your feet are parallel and shoulder-width apart. Your hands are on your lower belly with your right fist facing your belly. Tuck your tailbone forward and suck in your chest and belly to curve your back. At the same time, lower your left hand with fingers pointing to the Earth and open your right hand, raising it in front of the center of your body with the tip of your middle finger ending in front of your nose (Figure 10a and 10b). Then open your arms with your right hand drawing

Figure 10a

Figure 10b

an arch down to your right side and your left hand drawing an arch up to your left side. In the meantime, shift your weight to your right leg (Figure 11). Then lightly shift your weight to your left leg and continue drawing the arches with your hands until your right hand drops down to the front of your lower belly and your left hand is in front of your chest (Figure 12). Then take a big step to your right side, ending with your right knee bent and your left leg stretched. Then place your left hand on your left hip and raise your right hand, drawing an arch to your right side and ending with your middle finger at the same level as your eyebrow above your right foot (Figure 13).

Visualization: Imagine your fingers touching the end of the universe when you draw the arches. Imagine you are standing in a very stable stance on a boat and shifting right and left with the swelling of the waves when you shift your weight to right and left.

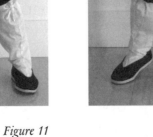

Figure 11

Figure 12

Figure 13

Function: In Chinese shamanic tradition, the feet are the very important root of your life energy and your spirit. We might find it difficult to step out or think about things if our energy is very weak. We always emphasize stability with each step or stance we take during the traditional cultivation. As we say in shamanic training, "As above, so below." We often use the feet as a tool to wake up our spiritual bodies to reach Shenming (spiritual brightness). Continuing this practice will enhance your life energy and lift up your spirit.

We finished our discussion early today. Hiking in the woods would be a wise choice for spending the rest of the day. We have several nice hiking trails here, and I am sure you will enjoy your hiking. Then you will have a good rest tonight.

My daily schedule might be irregular to you, and I hope it doesn't confuse you too much. You'll soon get used to my chaotic schedule. Irregular is the regular way! How about meeting at 9:00 a.m. tomorrow?

XUN 巽—

DAY **5**

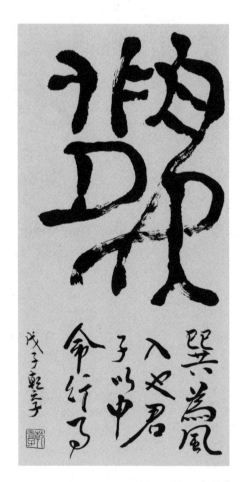

Xun (wind)

Ji shu zhi lai zhi wei zhan

極數知來之謂占

Using the number to understand the future is called divination.[1]

1　*Yijing. Xici* (*Appended Statements*). See *Zhouyi Shangshixue* (Beijing: Zhonghua Shuju, 1988: 291).

5. Zhan 占

The Divination

Divination or prediction played an important role in ancient China. Excavated materials from the Shang dynasty (1600–1027 BCE) and Zhou dynasty (1027–256 BCE) show us that kings or emperors always needed to do a divination before an

Zhan (divination)

important event. These divinations were all related to numerical calculation. If we want to know the ancient knowledge of Yi 易, we have to master two things:

1. Number—We need to understand the transition from a number to a Gua (trigram or hexagram) because this is the key to the divination method.

2. Symbol—After we determine the Gua from the number, we need to understand the symbolic meaning of the Gua and its interpreting system.[2]

QI GUA 起卦: MAKE A TRIGRAM WITH A NUMBER

It is another nice sunny day for us. I open the window on the southeast side of the tea house so that we have the tender breeze for company. I prepare the Zhuyeqing 竹葉青 (Bamboo Leaf Green) tea for us today. This is a rare kind of green tea from eastern China. The tea leaf is two or three times larger than regular green tea leaves but it is narrower and looks like a bamboo leaf. Also, I have prepared the tea in a clear glass tea set today. I pour the tea into these two small clear glass teacups so that we can see the color of the tea in a different way. The cup looks like a green crystal with this deep green tea in it. I ask you to take a cup and then I pick up a cup with three fingers, turn my wrist inward, and bring it close to my mouth. I look at the color of the tea again, and then I take a deep breath to bring the tea fragrance into my body. Next, I take three sips of the tea. I relax my eyelids and bring my eyesight within to feel the Qi of this tea.

I hope the hiking you did yesterday has enhanced your energy. We need good energy for today's discussion because it might be a little intense. Are you ready to learn how to make a trigram with a number?

Actually, the way of making a trigram is fairly easy. Here are the three basic steps to begin the Baguan Yuce (Eight Trigrams Divination):

1. Take a deep breath; relax your eyelids to look within. Feel your mind connect with your body. Next, think about the question or situation on which you want to consult. Then meditate on it and think about a three-digit number. When the number comes into your mind, write it down.

2. Divide this number by eight. Write down the remainder. If there is no remainder, please write down the number eight as the remainder.

---

2   Li, Ling. *Zhongguo Fangshu Kao* (Beijing: Dongfang Chubanshe, 2000: 260).

3. Use the number to find the trigram using the Prenatal Trigrams Arrangement Numbers. You will get the trigram Qian/Heaven if you get a remainder number 1; number 2 is the trigram Dui/Lake; number 3 is the trigram Li/Fire; number 4 is the trigram Zhen/Thunder; number 5 is the trigram Xun/Wind; number 6 is the trigram Kan/Water; number 7 is the trigram Gen/Mountain; and number 8 is the trigram Kun/Earth. Here is the reference table:

Remainder	1	2	3	4	5	6	7	8/0
Trigram	☰	☱	☲	☳	☴	☵	☶	☷
Chinese Name	Qian 乾	Dui 兑	Li 離	Zhen 震	Xun 巽	Kan 坎	Gen 艮	Kun 坤
English Name	Heaven	Lake	Fire	Thunder	Wind	Water	Mountain	Earth

Let us begin with an example. In the late afternoon on November 14, 2007, I met with a publisher to talk about publishing this *Yijing* prediction book. She asked me, "Do you use yarrow sticks or three coins to do the prediction?" "Neither of them," I said. "What do you do?" she asked again. "I need only a three-digit number for my *Yijing* consultation," I said. She responded immediately, "115." It took me a couple of seconds to get the remainder number 3 after I divided 115 by 8 in my mind. Number 3 indicates the trigram Li (Fire).

The answer for her question then is the trigram for Fire. At that moment, one of the symbolic meanings of the trigram Li, the word spirit, jumped into my mind. Then I said, "Your question is related to spirituality. If you give me your question, I can give you some details of the answer." "It is about a business that is related to spiritual cultivation," she confirmed.

Here is another example from my Intensive Taiji Workshop on December 10, 2007. Anna gave us the number 638. Please try to divide 638 by 8 to find the corresponding trigram. I take a sip of the Zhuyeqing tea while you do the calculation.

I'm sure that you got the remainder number 6, so it is the trigram Kan/Water. Think about it. What possible element is related to her question? Of course, her question has to do with Water.

You may wonder why we use a three-digit number to make the trigram. As we discussed on Day 1, trinity is the way of the universe. Regardless of whether an object is huge or minuscule, we can always measure it with three: the upper layer, middle layer, and lower layer. When we talk about time, no matter whether it is a long time or a short time, we can always measure it with three: past, present, and future. Therefore, a three-digit number is good enough to represent everything— and everything, whether it's an object, a phenomenon, or an idea, must be related to a number once it has been formed. We can use a three-digit number to manifest it. Also, there must be a trigram related to this number.

You may also wonder why we divide this number by the number 8. The reason for using the number 8 is that the Prenatal Trigrams Arrangement has 8 trigrams, and we should be able to categorize anything into one of these Eight Trigrams. The remainder indicates its quality.

As we discussed on Day 2, the Prenatal Eight Trigrams Arrangement stands for the Great Primordial Cosmos before creation, a being before birth (the prenatal time), or anything before it is formed or comes into existence. When we do the consultation, we need to find the root answer, the origin of the situation or problem, for our question. The prenatal trigram indicates the source of the answer. This is the reason we use the Xiantian Bagua (Prenatal Eight Trigrams Arrangement) to find the trigram rather than using the Houtian Bagua (Postnatal Eight Trigrams Arrangement). Certainly, we need to use the Houtian Bagua (Postnatal Eight Trigrams Arrangement) when we try to decode the answer from a trigram. The answer is in this arrangement because the Postnatal Arrangement represents the cosmos after creation, a person after birth, or an existing object.

It is easy to find a Gua for a question during the *Yijing* consultation. The difficult part is how to decode the correct answer to the question from the Gua. Please have a couple of cups of the Zhuyeqing tea and take three deep breaths with the breeze before we begin the decoding process.

JIE GUA 解卦: DECODE THE TRIGRAM

In my personal experience, the *Yijing* prediction system is still good enough to use in modern times. In fact, we use it in healing work, and people use it widely in their daily lives, such as to predict investments in the stock market. Sometimes, I still get phone calls from my friends in China asking for help with their important business decisions through my *Yijing* consultation.

Can you imagine how the ancient system might make predictions about modern life? Did ancient shamans know about modern objects?

Of course, ancient shamans did not know about modern objects, and they didn't list any of the modern items when they talked about the symbolic meanings of the Bagua (Eight Trigrams). However, they did show us how to find the connection between an object and a trigram. The spirit of *Yijing* is the Yi (Change). The objects and topics of our life are quite different from ancient times, but we can still classify everything with one of the symbolic meanings of the Bagua if we truly understand the ancient system. Also, this knowledge of the symbolic meanings is a great foundation for becoming a predictor. This is the reason we should learn the symbolic meanings of the Bagua (Eight Trigrams).

Please remember that you **never decode a trigram in a mechanical way** in your *Yijing* consultation even though we have to talk about it mechanically at first. Are you ready to begin the process of trigram interpretation?

Resonate with the symbolic meanings. You should be very relaxed to allow your heart to resonate with the symbolic meanings of the trigram after you have made a trigram from the three-digit number. These resonated meanings should be very close to the answer to the question. Even if you intellectually try to find the symbolic meanings to the question, you should narrow down the information that is related to the question. Otherwise, you might get lost in the consultation because each trigram holds so much information. Here is an example from my Intensive Taiji Workshop on December 10, 2007:

Adriana gave the **number** 946. We divided it by 8 and got the **remainder number** 2. The **Corresponding Trigram** is Dui/Lake. Then I asked, "What is your question?" She said, "Should my grandmother have surgery on her bladder?" I answered right away, "Definitely, yes."

Of course, the trigram Dui has many symbolic meanings: joy, mouth, shaman, young woman, lake, and more. But at that moment, the symbolic meanings of Dui that jumped into my mind were "break" and "knife" and this information definitely points to an answer for the surgery. We can intellectually analyze more information that will be related to the question about surgery on the bladder: Dui is in the west, which represents Western medicine/hospital in this case, so it will be good for her grandmother to go to the hospital for bladder surgery. Dui corresponds to the Metal element and the bladder is a Water element organ. Metal gives birth to Water; therefore, the surgery

(Metal) will benefit the Water (bladder). In this case, the above analysis is good enough for the answer, so it is not necessary to delve into more details of the symbolic meanings of Dui/Lake.

Here is another example from the same workshop:

> Katherine gave the **number** 364. We divided it by 8 and got the **remainder number** 4. The **Corresponding Trigram** is Zhen/Thunder. Then I asked, "What is your question?" She answered, "What time of year is best to leave my [acupuncture] practice?" I said, "Next spring."

> In this case, if you remember the symbolic meanings we discussed yesterday, the answer is so easy. The trigram Zhen gives us a very clear answer because Zhen is the symbol for moving, and Zhen represents spring from a time perspective. It would only confuse us if we tried to get more symbolic meanings of the trigram Zhen when the symbolic season fits our answer so well. The answer should be tied directly to the question.

Figure out the prenatal and postnatal positions. When you have the trigram, you should figure out where it is located in the Prenatal Eight Trigrams Arrangement and in the Postnatal Eight Trigrams Arrangement and the related trigrams in these positions. These positions may help you find a better answer in your consultation because the prenatal position stands for the root of a situation, and the postnatal stands for the present or future direction.

Let us go through the Eight Trigrams first. Now, you can take out the lists of the prenatal and postnatal arrangements details from our discussion on Day 2 if you can't remember all the details. The trigram Qian/Heaven in the prenatal position is south and the related trigram is Li/Fire because Li/Fire takes over the south position in the postnatal arrangement. Qian/Heaven in the postnatal position is northwest and the related trigram is Gen/Mountain because Qian/Heaven takes over Gen/Mountain's prenatal position in the postnatal arrangement. For the same reason, the trigram Dui/Lake's prenatal position is southeast and the related trigram is Xun/Wind; its postnatal position is west and the related trigram is Kan/Water. The prenatal position of the trigram Li/Fire is east and the related trigram is Zhen/Thunder; its postnatal position is south and the related trigram is Qian/Heaven. The prenatal position of the trigram Zhen/Thunder is northeast and the related trigram is Gen/Mountain; its postnatal position is east and the related trigram is Li/Fire. The prenatal position of the trigram Xun/Wind is southwest and the related trigram is Kun/Earth; its postnatal position is southeast and the related trigram is Dui/Lake. The prenatal position of the trigram Kan/ Water is west and the related trigram is Dui/Lake; its postnatal position is north and the related trigram is Kun/Earth. The prenatal position of the trigram Gen/ Mountain is northwest and the related trigram is Qian/Heaven; its postnatal position is northeast and the related trigram is Zhen/Thunder. The prenatal position of the trigram Kun/Earth is north and the related trigram is Kan/Water; its postnatal position is southwest and the related trigram is Xun/Wind. Here is the reference table:

Remainder	1	2	3	4	5	6	7	8/0
Trigram	Qian Heaven	Dui Lake	Li Fire	Zhen Thunder	Xun Wind	Kan Water	Gen Mountain	Kun Earth
Prenatal Location /Related Trigram	south /Li	southeast /Xun	east /Zhen	northeast /Gen	southwest /Kun	west /Dui	northwest /Qian	north /Kan
Postnatal Location /Related Trigram	northwest /Gen	west /Kan	south /Qian	east /Li	southeast /Dui	north /Kun	northeast /Zhen	southwest /Xun

Here is an example of working with location from my Intensive Taiji Workshop on December 10, 2007:

> Keivan gave the **number** 711. We divided it by 8 and got the **remainder number** 7. The **Corresponding Trigram** is Gen/Mountain. Then I asked, "What is your question?" He said, "Where is a good location to move my clinic (regarding whether or not to join with a potential partner)?" My answer was, "Since Gen is in the northeast corner of the postnatal arrangement, the best move would be to the northeast; it will be stable." The conversation continued: "How about northwest?" "It will not be good to move to the northwest where the potential partner is."

> In this case, the northeast location of the trigram Gen represents the present and future for the answer. The northwest is the prenatal position of Gen, and it represents the past. It means Keivan's profession was related to the northwest area, and it would be good if he had practiced there before but the energy is shifting to the northeast, and he should move to that direction even if he loses the potential partner.

Let us change the tea leaves and make a new pot of tea. Try this Anji 安吉 (Peaceful Auspicious) white tea from my home province Zhejiang in southeast China. This tea leaf is a green color. I put a good amount of tea leaves into the teapot, and then I pour in the hot water. Please look carefully at these tea leaves. After they have steeped for a few seconds, the color of the tea leaves gets lighter and lighter. I pour the tea into the cups; the fragrance is gentle and smooth and makes me feel so relaxed. This tea is good for liver cleansing and body purification. Help yourself. Now we can look at another case from the same workshop:

> Michael gave the **number** 585. We divided it by 8 and got the **remainder number** 1. So the **Corresponding Trigram** is Qian/Heaven. Then he gave us this question, "How should I deal with a troubled relationship with someone? Let it lie or work it out?" I said, "It is worth working it out. The problem came from stagnation in communication."

In this case, the trigram Qian represents the communication, and it indicates that he should work out the problem through communication. The postnatal position of Qian is northwest where the trigram Gen/Mountain is located in

Anji tea

the prenatal arrangement. This shows that the original problem is related to the trigram Gen. Gen represents stagnation or stubbornness, so the problem comes from stubbornness and lack of communication.

Let us look at one more case from the same workshop that is also related to the northwest direction:

Erica gave the **number** 857. We divided it by 8 and got the **remainder number** 1. So the **Corresponding Trigram** is Qian/Heaven. Then she asked, "Where is the best place for me to practice?" Of course, my answer was "In the northwest."

In this case, since Qian is in the northwest position in the postnatal arrangement, the best place for her to practice is in the northwest area of her location. And it would also be good if her office faced northwest. In general, when we talk about the location direction, it means any place that is more than one hundred yards away from the center of your birthplace or where you live now. You don't have to move from the East Coast to the Pacific Northwest if you get the trigram Qian for your future location prediction.

It might help you get many more details of the answer during your consultation if you understand very well the Five Elements quality of each trigram and the Five Elements principle. Now I can feel the cleansing function of the Anji white tea within my body. Let us take a short "water break" before we go through the Five Elements.

EIGHT TRIGRAMS AND FIVE ELEMENTS

Wuxing 五行, the Five Elements theory, is the essence of classical Chinese philosophy. In Chinese, Wu 五 means five and the oracle bone style for Wu is a symbol to represent the Yin and Yang energies interacting and dancing between Heaven and Earth. This is the pattern of peace, balance, and health. Xing 行 means intersection, element, phase, movement, act, path, career, and good. The oracle bone style for Xing looks like a pattern of intersection, and it is a symbol that stands for connection, communication, and circulation. This pattern represents a harmonious community or world.

In Wu 巫 (Chinese shamanic) cosmology, the three layers of the universe are constructed of Wuxing, the Five Elements of Water, Fire, Wood, Metal, and Earth. Each element contains its own characteristic Qi, and a natural cycle exists

Wu (five)

Xing (element)

through which the Qi of one element is transformed into another. Peace and harmony exist when the Qi of the Five Elements flows freely through this cycle. The Five Elements do not merely refer to Water, Wood, Fire, Earth, and Metal. The word that is translated as "element" here actually means movement, change, or development. Each movement has its Yin and Yang aspect and each should be in balance. In a balanced environment, one will live peacefully and feel lucky.

In the *Yijing* prediction system, each trigram has the Five Elements quality. Understanding the Five Elements principle and the trigram's relationship with Five Elements is an important way to mastering the prediction system.

Shui Huo 水火: Hidden Talisman Water and Thunder Dragon Fire

We need to be very clear about the Five Elements quality of each trigram. Let us take a couple of minutes to review this.

The trigram Qian belongs to the Metal element; Dui belongs to the Metal element, and it also has the Water element hidden within. We call this Water Yinfushui 陰符水, which means Hidden Talisman Water. This represents one of the Five Elements principles: Jinshuyijia 金水一家, which means Metal and Water are one family.

Li belongs to the Fire element; Zhen belongs to the Wood element, and it also has the Fire element hidden within. We call this Fire Leilonghuo 雷龍火, which means Thunder Dragon Fire, and this represents one of the Five Elements principles: Muhuoyijia 木火一家, which means Wood and Fire are one family.

Xun belongs to the Wood element; Kan belongs to the Water element; Gen belongs to the Earth element; and Kun belongs to the Earth element. As you can see, each element has two trigrams associated with it to represent the Yin and Yang quality of the element.

The Metal element has Qian and Dui; the Water element has Kan and Dui; the Wood element has Zhen and Xun; the Fire element has Li and Zhen; and the Earth element has Kun and Gen. Here is the reference table:

Trigram	Qian ☰	Dui ☱	Li ☲	Zhen ☳	Xun ☴	Kan ☵	Gen ☶	Kun ☷
Element	Metal	Metal/ Water	Fire	Wood/ Fire	Wood	Water	Earth	Earth
Yin/Yang	Yang	Yin	Yin	Yang	Yin	Yang	Yang	Yin

Let me tell you about a case that is related to using the above information:

> On September 4, 2007, during my Lifelong Training session, Diana asked, "What should I be doing to help my back pain?" After doing the calculation, we got the remainder number 2 for the trigram Dui/Lake. Because Dui is the Yin Metal element, which represents Lung, and Dui also has the hidden element Yin Water, which represents Kidney, this information indicates that her back pain is related to weakness in her Lung and Kidney functions. So, she needs to strengthen her Lung and Kidney functions instead of just working with the back pain.

Sheng Ke 生克: Generating and Controlling Cycles

We should remember two cycles in the Five Elements principles: Sheng 生 (Generating Cycle) and Ke 克 (Controlling Cycle). In the Generating Cycle, one element gives birth to another element.

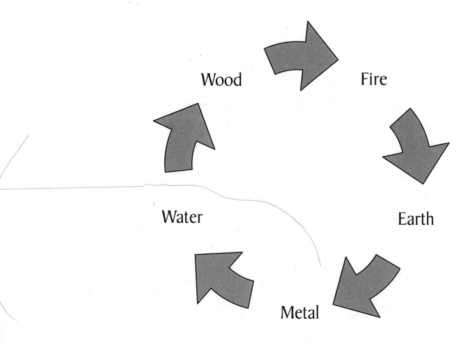

If we start with the Metal element, then Metal gives birth to Water, Water gives birth to Wood, Wood gives birth to Fire, Fire gives birth to Earth, and Earth gives birth to Metal. In this relationship, the element that gives birth leaks energy, and the generated element increases energy. For example, when Metal gives birth to Water, the Metal reduces energy, but the Water gains energy. During your prediction, you need to figure out whether the energy of the element for your answer needs to be reduced or increased. The answer will be positive if the element fits what you need. Otherwise, the answer will be negative. Let us revisit Michael's case:

> As you recall, Michael gave the **number** 585. We divided it by 8 and got the **remainder number** 1. So, the **Corresponding Trigram** is Qian/Heaven. Then he gave us this question: "How should I deal with a troubled relationship with someone? Let it lie or work it out?" I said, "It is worthwhile to work it out. The problem came from stagnation in communication."
>
> In this case, the trigram Qian represents the communication, and it indicates that he should work out the problem through communication. The postnatal position of Qian is northwest where the trigram Gen is located in the prenatal arrangement. This shows that the original problem is related to the trigram Gen. Gen represents stagnation or stubbornness, so the problem came from stubbornness and lack of communication.

Actually, you will see more clearly the reason I gave him a positive answer for working out the relationship if we look at the Five Elements relationship between the trigrams Gen and Qian. Gen is the Earth element and it represents the stagnation problem in this case, so it would be good to take the stagnation away and let the energy flow. The trigram Qian is the Metal element, and it represents the communication in this case. Earth gives birth to Metal, so Metal (the communication) could take away the energy from Earth (the problem).

According to the same principle of Earth giving birth to Metal, a negative answer was determined for the northwest direction in Keivan's question. Let us review his case:

> Keivan gave the **number** 711. We divided it by 8 and got the **remainder number** 7. The **Corresponding Trigram** is Gen/Mountain. Then I asked, "What is your question?" He said, "Where is a good location to move my clinic (regarding whether or not to join with a potential partner)?" My answer was, "Since Gen is in the northeast corner of the postnatal arrangement, the

best move would be to the northeast; it will be stable." Then he asked, "How about northwest?" My reply was, "It will not be good to move to the northwest where the potential partner is."

In this case, the northeast location of the trigram Gen/Mountain represents the present and future time of the answer. The northwest is the prenatal position of Gen and it represents the past, meaning that Keivan's profession was related to the northwest area and it would have been good if he had practiced there before. But the energy is shifting to the northeast, and he should move to that direction even if he loses the potential partner.

In this case, Gen represents the stability of the business and finances, and it needs to be supported and not have its energy taken away. The northwest Metal element would take away energy from Gen. This indicates that he would lose his business in the northwest area if he moved there.

In the Controlling Cycle, one element controls another element.

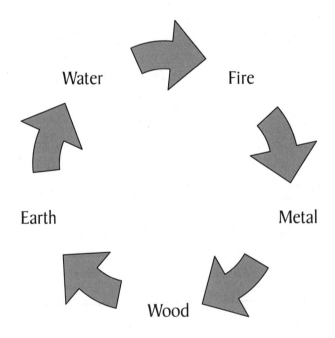

Let us begin with the Metal element again. Metal controls Wood, Wood controls Earth, Earth controls Water, Water controls Fire, and Fire controls Metal. A controlling element takes energy to control, refine, or weaken the energy of its controlled element. A controlled element takes energy to cooperate or resist against its controlling element. The answer will be positive if the result of these elements balances the situation in the question; otherwise, the answer will be negative. As I described earlier, an interesting case occurred at one of my Lifelong Training sessions when we helped Jack find his lost dog. After calculating the corresponding trigram Kun/Earth from the number 648 Jack gave us and considering the symbolic meanings of the trigram, we came up with a number of ideas about how to find the dog. One, as the trigram Kun is related to the belly, the dog might have been hungry and moved in the southwest direction to find food. Two, since the prenatal location of southwest is the trigram Xun and the symbolic meaning of Xun is wind, which could represent the news on the air, it might help to make an announcement on the local radio. Three, the dog could be on the southwest side of the house where there is a piece of flat land. After about a half hour of discussing this case I felt that the dog was definitely on the southwest side of Jack's house. I persuaded Jack to call his wife and he reported back to the group that his wife had found their dog in a barn on the southwest side of the house where there is a large piece of flat land. His wife had looked in the barn earlier and didn't see him, but while we were in the midst of our discussion, she checked the barn and found the dog inside.

In this case, everyone figured out the southwest direction because this is the postnatal location of the trigram Kun, and the postnatal location represents the current situation. The trigram Xun is located in the southwest in the prenatal trigrams arrangement, and it represents the source of the answer. Xun belongs to the Wood element and Kun belongs to the Earth element. Wood controls Earth, so the dog should be found in the southwest and should be fine. The result was that the barn (Wood) held the dog (Earth).

Liu Qin 六親: Relationships

In Chinese, Liu 六 means six and Qin 親 means relative. In general, a person has six different types of relatives, so we use Liu Qin to talk about relatives and friendship. We also use Liu Qin to represent the different relationships between two elements in our *Yijing* prediction. Actually, this information contains the details of the relationships among elements from the Controlling Cycle and Generating Cycle. Here is the information.

Let us assume you are a certain element. We call the element that gives birth to you Fumu 父母, which means father and mother. Fumu indicates the information of parents, education, paperwork, food, or clothing. The element that you give birth to we call Zisun 子孫, children and grandchildren. Zisun indicates the information of children, medication, healing, or good luck. We call the element that controls you Guangui 官鬼, officer and ghost. Guangui indicates the information of grandparents, boss, husband, lawsuit, or bad luck. The element that you control we call Qicai 妻財, wife and finance. Qicai indicates the information of wife, salary, finance, house, and realtor. If the element is the same element as you, we call it Xiongdi 兄弟, brother and sister. Xiongdi indicates the information of brother, sister, friends, or business partner. For instance, if you are the Metal element, then the Earth element is your Fumu, father and mother; the Water element is your Zisun, children and grandchildren; the Fire element is your Guangui, officer and ghost; the Wood element is your Qicai, wife and finance; and the other Metal element is your Xiongdi, brother and sister. Here is the reference table:

Relationship / Element	Fumu 父母 father, mother	Zisun 子孫 children, grandchildren	Guangui 官鬼 officer, ghost	Qicai 妻財 wife, finance	Xiongdi 兄弟 brother, sister
Fire	Wood	Earth	Water	Metal	Fire
Earth	Fire	Metal	Wood	Water	Earth
Metal	Earth	Water	Fire	Wood	Metal
Water	Metal	Wood	Earth	Fire	Water
Wood	Water	Fire	Metal	Earth	Wood

Let us review Katherine's case:

> Katherine gave the **number** 364. We divided it by 8 and got the **remainder number** 4. So the **Corresponding Trigram** is Zhen/Thunder. Then I asked, "What is your question?" She answered, "What time of year is best to leave my [acupuncture] practice?" I said, "Next spring."

In this case, the trigram Zhen gives us the very clear answer of spring. It also indicates that the move will be good for Katherine's business if we look at the Liu Qin relationship. Zhen is located in the northeast in the prenatal arrangement, which is the trigram Gen/Mountain in the postnatal position. Zhen is the Wood element and Gen is the Earth element. Wood controls Earth, so Earth is the Qicai (wife and finance) of the Wood, which indicates that the move will improve her financial situation and the northeast area will be the better choice.

Jin Tui 進退: Develop and Decline

Develop and Decline is an advanced prediction technique that is related to timing. This technique will help you to figure out when the outcome of your inquiry will happen. The Chinese character Jin 進 means forward, progress, and develop. In the Five Elements principle, we use it to represent the developing stage of an element. For instance, if the Wood element is in the late winter or early spring, we consider this Wood element to be in the Jin, developing stage, because Wood energy will get stronger and stronger during the spring season. The Chinese character Tui 退 means backward, withdraw, and decline. In the Five Elements principle, we use it to represent the declining stage of an element. For instance, if the Wood element is in the late spring or summer, we consider this Wood element to be in the Tui, declining stage, because Wood energy will get weaker and weaker as the spring season ends and summer begins. If the element of your inquiry is in the Jin (developing stage), it indicates that the energy of this subject is getting strong and the outcome will happen soon. If the element of your inquiry is in the Tui, declining stage, it indicates that the energy of this inquiry is getting weak and the outcome will happen late or may not happen at all.

Do you remember the dog story in Jack's case (see pp.30–31)? The reason I said, "Your wife might have found the dog already" is that the corresponding trigram Kun belongs to the Earth element, and the time we were discussing this case was the beginning of one of the Earth element times (7:00–9:00 p.m. or 8:00–10:00 p.m. Daylight Saving Time), so the subject was in the Jin, developing stage, and the outcome should happen soon.

If you want to understand more details of the *Yijing* prediction skills, you should take more time to learn how to figure out the elements of a year, month/season, day, and time.

Ti Yong 體用: Body and Function

We will not talk too much about the information of the Ti Yong prediction technique because we will not have enough time to discuss its prediction application in this eight-day course. However, it will be very useful to learn this if you want to do detailed predictions in the future. For now, let us just look briefly at the concept. The Chinese Character Ti 體 means body, and it represents the subject of the prediction. The Chinese character Yong 用 means function, employ, and utilize. It represents the activity of the subject and its environmental aspects. If you do advanced *Yijing* predictions in the future, you should figure out which elements your subject Ti belongs to. Also, you should figure out Yong, which elements the activity of the subject and its environmental aspects belong to. It will be a positive effect to the answer if the Yong makes Ti balanced, and it will be a negative effect to the answer if the Yong makes Ti unbalanced.

We have covered a lot of information today. It will become easy for you to work with this information if you practice prediction every day. We will play with this again in tomorrow's discussion. Let us go to the bamboo garden to practice the Taiji Qigong now.

TAIJI QIGONG XUN 巽 (WIND)

It feels calm and peaceful in this bamboo garden. I take a deep breath and bring my eyesight back to my body, then listen with my body to the music from the bamboo leaves, birds, and the little stream nearby. After several minutes of silence, we start reviewing the practice of Taiji Qigong Qian, Dui, Li, and Zhen. I feel my body becoming part of the gentle breeze after slowly repeating these movements eight times. Then we start our new practice: Xun.

Movement: Now start from the last posture, the Zhen practice. Shift your weight to your left, keeping your right leg straight and left knee bent while you turn your left hand to the center of your body and bring your right hand to the center in front of your body (Figure 14). Shift your weight to your right leg and drop your right hand down to your right side (Figure 15). Bring your left foot close to your right foot. In the meantime, raise your left hand through the center in front of your body, ending with your middle fingertip in front of the tip of your nose. Then turn over your left hand with palm facing forward. Raise your right hand as if you are drawing an arch to your right side, ending with your middle finger at the same level as your eyebrow at the right side of your forehead. (Figure 16).

Figure 14

Visualization: Imagine your fingers touching the end of the universe when you draw the arches and feel your arms are like big wings spreading at the same time. Imagine yourself like a giant swan opening its wings and standing very stable on the ground in the ending posture.

Function: Swans understand the current of the wind, and they know when the time is right to fly and then they will fly. When it is time for rest, they will rest. Actually, this movement is imitating the spirit of the swan. This practice will help us move into a peaceful and harmonious state.

Figure 15

I hope you will enjoy the rest of this sunny day by spending time in Nature. It will be rainy tomorrow and it may snow. We can start our discussion at 11:00 p.m. tomorrow night, but you could come over to my cabin for dinner at 6:00 p.m. if you would like. I will prepare a special "Wu-style" Chinese pork dish during the rainy and snowy day. I'll use my own secret recipe for the pork dish. I will prepare plenty of food for us. You may bring some Guinness beer if you'd like. Please come at 6:00 p.m. tomorrow.

Figure 16

KAN 坎—

DAY 6

Kan (water)

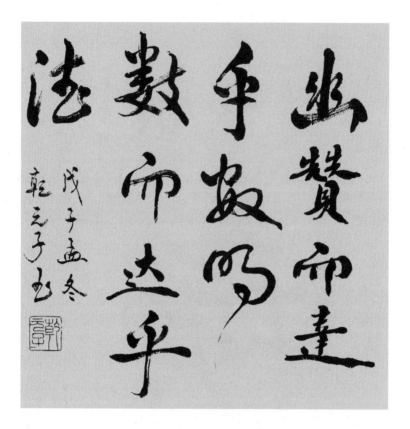

You Zan er da hu shu, ming shu er da hu de

幽贊而達乎數, 明數而達乎德

Intuiting the Zan 赞 *(ancient shamanic ritual) to reach the number, and understanding the number to reach the virtue (function).*

Confucius, *Yao* 要 *(Essentials), from Mawangdui Silk Book*[1]

---

1   The *Mawangdui Silk Book* was discovered in the tomb of Li Cang (d. 168 BCE) at Mawangdui, in Changsha, Hunan, China. It was translated into English by Edward L.Shaughnessy. See *I Ching (The Book of Change)* (New York: Ballantine Publishing Group, 1997: 240).

6. Li 例

Case Analyses

In my personal experience, I have found one of the best ways to improve the prediction skill is through case study. With each prediction case, you should analyze what you did in your process and try to figure out why you got the right answers in some predictions and where you went wrong in others. Also, you should spend much time studying other people's prediction cases so you can learn from their experiences, especially in the beginning stage of your *Yijing* prediction study.

In today's discussion, I will present some cases. Most of these cases were done in my classes, and some came from my students' practice. I will try to set out different types of cases here, but you'll notice that a number of them are related to health or healing questions. This is because many of my students are health practitioners.

Li (case)

145

PORK STEW

It is nice that we had some snow this afternoon. The ground is still covered with a few inches of snow, and it makes the whole land so pure and fresh. I open my door for you, and then you bring the cold air along with your Guinness into the cabin. I take a deep breath to suck in the cold fresh Qi from outside before I close the door.

Are you hungry now? The food is ready. We sit at the small round dining table. The food is simple. The main dish, a pot of pork stew, is in the middle of the table. We have squid fired with fresh hot pepper, garlic, snow peas, and carrots, all surrounded by fresh lettuce leaves.

The pork is so delicious. Would you like to know my secret recipe? Actually, the recipe is easy. You need pork belly, garlic, green onion, star anise, cinnamon, sugar, soy sauce, red wine, and olive oil. The cooking process is complicated and takes six hours. Please try this fatty part. This big piece looks scary but it is the best part! The meat will melt in your mouth, and you will have a nice moist feeling instead of an oily feeling. The six hours of cooking makes the difference. It is the same in the *Yijing* study; you will be good at it if you could spend enough time to "stew" the knowledge in your inner cauldron. Eat as much as you want. I have prepared a couple of pounds of the pork for us. It will be very good for your Kidney and brain.

You may wonder why this pork dish is good for the brain. Remember that the pig is the animal related with the trigram Kan/Water; so on the energetic level, pork energy will be good for the Kidney function. In Chinese medicine, we call the brain the Bone Marrow Ocean. Kidney is in charge of the bone marrow; therefore, your brain function is rooted in the Kidney. Your brain function will not work well if the Kidney is weak. In general, the pork energy is fairly Yin, so we take six hours to stew it to refine the energy, which will tonify your Kidney and your brain.

Here is a story related to the connection between the brain and Kidney. Just a few days ago, my friend and student David came to the cabin and asked me which Qigong form he should teach his friend Kate because she has senile dementia. I said Kate needs to strengthen her Kidney because the problem of her brain not functioning well is caused by a Kidney problem. Then I told him to teach her some simple Qigong movements to strengthen her Kidney. And, interestingly, I figured out that Kate had kidney failure.

After the dinner, I am going to watch *The House of Flying Daggers* movie before our *Yijing* case study. You are welcome to watch the movie with me. This movie will help you deeply understand the Five Elements principles and love, especially in the spiritual level. You do not have to go back and review your notes before watching the movie. Just remember that everything is connected. You should find the connections among the different things and your answer during your prediction.

BURNING INCENSE AND HEART

We've just finished watching the movie, and it is now 11:00 p.m. It is bright outside. The silvery, transparent moonlight covers the snow and makes the ground look like a big piece of jade. I prepare my special Yueguangcha 月光茶 (Moonlight Tea) for us. Please look closely at the tea leaf. The leaf is big and three or four times wider than regular green tea leaves. One side of the leaf is dark, and the other side is covered with tiny silver hairs. It looks like a piece of shiny Chinese silk cloth. Essentially, the process of harvesting this tea is irregular. This tea is from the Yi 彝 minority in China. This minority still holds much ancient knowledge that is very close to ancient Chinese shamanism and Daoism. Some of the Yi elders still know the ancient cosmology, and they will guide people to pick the tea leaves from old-growth bushes during a certain time period and dehydrate them under the moonlight so the tea absorbs special Yin Qi from the moon. It contains almost no caffeine, but it can help your mind be calm and clear. It is good to drink after a heavy dinner. Here is the cup for you. I pick up my cup and take a deep breath with three sips, and I feel my whole body melt into the moonlight.

Now, please review a case from Suzanna's 2007 China Trip notes and the outcome. It is fairly long but it will give you an overview of a trigram prediction process and the detailed actual situation will help you understand it better:

Student: Suzanna

Number: 354

Corresponding Trigram: #2 Dui Lake

Question: How is Rocksanda?

Analysis: It was a steamy, hot day in Longquan, China. We were sitting inside the classroom going over the various methods of *Yijing* divination that could be applied in a medical context. In that session, we were taught how to use a three-digit number to calculate a trigram that would provide some special insight into the situation that we needed information about. In order to come up with a number, we meditated on a situation, question, or person and then allowed a three-digit number to arise in our minds.

Master Wu asked us if we had any situations that we would like to share as examples for the group. I thought of an old family friend named Rocksanda whom I had stayed with in New York before going to China. Rocksanda had mentioned that there was something wrong with her heart (a valve defect). She was on medication, and her Western doctors were encouraging her to have surgery. I immediately thought of her when we were asked if we had examples for the class. I meditated on her, visualizing her in my mind's eye, and asked for a number. I got the number 354.

I reported this to the group, and we calculated 354 divided by 8. We got 44 with a remainder of 2, which gave us the trigram Dui/Lake. I had not said anything about Rocksanda or the context of the case. All of the information that came up was from the divination. A dialogue among myself, Master Wu, and the rest of the class ensued that provided astonishingly accurate insight into Rocksanda's condition on the physical, mental, emotional, and energetic levels.

The first question Master Wu asked was if the person I was asking about was a young woman. (Dui is the youngest daughter.) Rocksanda is not young; in fact, she is in her early sixties, but she does have a markedly youthful quality about her in the way she dresses as well as in the way that she carries herself and behaves. Master Wu explained to us that the *Yijing* is not mechanical or literal, but that the idea of Dui as a young woman could refer more to an energetic quality than a physical or material one. After that, he asked if she was talkative. (Dui is mouth.) I had to say yes to this as she is one of the most talkative people I know. She is constantly talking in a very hurried, humorous manner. Being around her, one gets the feeling that silence makes her uncomfortable.

At this point, the conversation shifted to a discussion of her pathology. Master Wu was pacing around the front of the room and kicked over a coil of burning incense that was lying on the floor. He looked up and said that she had some problem with her Fire element, which in Chinese medicine includes the Heart. He said that the Fire element had expressed itself through his action of kicking Fire in the form of burning incense, and that since we were in the process of a divination concerning Rocksanda, the Fire element itself was directly relevant. This fascinated me because up until then, I had not really understood that aspect of *Yijing* divination; that is, the relevance of symbolic information coming in from the outside during this process. The Dui trigram actually symbolizes Metal, not Fire, so Master Wu posited that there must be a Metal problem (perhaps the Lung organ) affecting her Fire. This point I could not confirm but I do feel that she may have weak Metal because she has an underlying tendency towards depression.

Master Wu commented that she is the sort of person who appears happy on the surface but underneath there is sadness. Rocksanda has definitely suffered many losses in her life and struggles with finances as well. I could definitely confirm that statement about her.

At this point in the conversation, a man came into the room and offered us plum wine. It was perhaps the second or maybe even the third time that he had come in to ask us if we were ready to taste this wine made from plums grown in the area. After we politely told him we would like the wine with our dinner, he left the room and Master Wu said confidently, "This lady loves to drink wine." I might have laughed at this had it not been the truth. For Rocksanda, wine is almost a religion. I remember that one year my mother gave her a rubber wine stopper as a gift, thinking that because of her love of wine, she would use it often. It turned out that Rocksanda gave my mother the stopper back after a while, saying, "I don't use it. I never leave a bottle unfinished. Once I open one, I drink until there is no more wine left."

We moved on to talking more generally about Rocksanda and came up with the following qualities to describe her: she is sensitive, prone to issues with her shoulders and hips, and she has some underlying sadness because the trigram Dui represents broken energy. The sensitivity part is definitely true as Rocksanda is quite a wonderful pianist. Master Wu mentioned that the Metal element goes with music, so her being a musician makes sense. He also told us that there was a hidden element of Water in the Dui trigram reading. The hidden element of Water indicates that there might be an underlying issue with the Water organs, namely Kidney or Bladder, which could manifest in the future.

As a group, we decided that Rocksanda would benefit from strengthening her Metal element by sleeping with her head facing west, hanging a sword in her home, and doing more cultivation and meditation. Also, we thought that she should go easy on the wine. These prescriptions will be very difficult for Rocksanda to follow, particularly cutting down on the wine because it is an integral part of her life. She loves it and doesn't understand how cutting down would improve her Heart function. However, just the experience of using this *Yijing* diagnostic technique was in itself a great way to shed light on her situation. Hopefully, in time she will be more open to suggestions.

Outcome: To conclude, I followed up with Rocksanda a few months after having returned from China to get some more details on her condition. She told me that she has a mitral valve prolapse with severe mitral regurgitation. This makes her feel very tired with activity; she cannot walk as fast as she used to. She loses breath pretty easily in general. (This ties in nicely with our Metal-Fire diagnostic divination, as the Lung and Heart are both affected.) Her symptoms of low energy and shortness of breath have been worse in the last year and a half. When she is stressed out and cannot sleep, her symptoms are worse. She has a history of insomnia. Rocksanda's pathological picture, while multifaceted and complex, was ultimately illuminated by our *Yijing* diagnostic procedure.

Wu's Commentary: In this case, we focused on the corresponding trigram Dui/Lake without considering its related trigrams in the prenatal arrangement or postnatal arrangement. The important information in this case is the external environmental factors affecting the prediction. We call this prediction technique Waiying 外應, which literally means external responding or external resonance. Waiying should be a hint for your answer because any incident that occurs during the course of a prediction is important and you must recognize that it has occurred for a reason. We use this technique all the time in Yijing *prediction. You might get the same corresponding trigram or hexagram 30 times in 100 prediction cases, but the Waiying never happens in the same way if you observe it carefully during your prediction. In this case, I caught Waiying two times: I kicked over the burning incense, and the man tried to bring in plum wine for us several times during this prediction. These incidents were relevant to our prediction.*

Ying (responding)

The changes are the spirit of the *Yijing* prediction. When the time changes or the environment changes or the question changes, you should resonate different answers for your question even if you get the same corresponding trigram every time. Let us review more Dui/Lake cases. I hope these will bring you some inspiration.

THE MAGICAL MIRROR

I remember a spiritual fiction story I read when I was about ten years old. In the story, a shaman has a magical mirror that can show him the true face of everything, even a high-level spirit who has taken on a different face. In Chinese shamanic tradition, the mirror is a metaphor for the highly awakened consciousness. Each trigram can be the magical mirror in the prediction if our consciousness can truly resonate with it. Let us review a Dui/Lake case from my Intensive Taiji Workshop on December 10, 2007:

Student: Helga

Number: 842

Corresponding Trigram: #2 Dui/Lake

Question: Should I change my daughter's preschool?

Analysis: If she wants to change her daughter's preschool, she could go to the west (of her house or the city). Since Dui is about speech, joyfulness, openness, and communication, the present problem could be about communication with the school and the teachers. There may be some gossip about her daughter's teacher. However, since the current school is northeast of her house, it corresponds to the trigram Gen/Mountain, which works well with Dui/Lake. Because of this, it would also be fine to stay.

Outcome: Helga had heard some gossip about the teacher, and this had made her question whether her daughter should stay there.

Wu's Commentary: In this case, we got the answer through comparing the Five Elements relationship between the corresponding trigram Dui/Lake and the location of the school. In general, assume your location is in the center and figure out the location of the other object. Then check the Postnatal Trigrams Arrangement to find the related trigram. In this case, the object (school) is located northeast of her house, and northeast is the position of the trigram Gen/Mountain in the postnatal arrangement. Gen/Mountain is the Earth element, and it gives birth to the Metal element of Dui/Lake, which will be good for education, so the answer is that it would be better to stay.

Let us take a look at Diana's Dui/Lake case from my Lifelong Training session again:

Student: Diana

Number: 586

Corresponding Trigram: #2 Dui/Lake

Question: What should I be doing to help my back pain?

Analysis: Dui/Lake is the Yin Metal element, which represents the Lung, and also has the hidden element Yin/Water, which represents the Kidney Water. Dui/Lake in the prenatal position is southeast, which is related with the trigram Xun/Wind, and it represents the Liver and blood systems. Therefore, this is a blood system problem. Also, it is a Water system problem. Dui is the Metal element and Metal is the mother of Water. Supporting Metal will tonify the Water element. The Lungs need to be supported because Lung belongs to the Metal element. Lungs are also related to grief. Bringing some joy into your life is the positive energy of the trigram Dui. Specifically, chanting with water, meditating with water, using herbs that tonify Qi and blood, visiting sacred sites, and singing songs that bring you joy will be beneficial.

Outcome: Three months after the retreat, I got feedback from Diana: "I've been sick a lot with Lung disorders, but my debilitating chronic back pain has been gone since the retreat in September, and I've done the Taiji form every day."

Wu's Commentary: Diana's feedback indicates that her back pain was related to her Lung weakness. The back pain symptom disappeared as a result of her Qigong and Taiji practice, but the root of the back pain—the Lung problem—occurred. In the Qi energetic healing process, the root problem of a symptom will be naturally brought out if you practice Taiji Qigong every day at a deep level, and you should understand the process to work out the root problem. She still needs to strengthen her Lung function through the Taiji Qigong. Again, the sadness and grief energy in her life will weaken the Lung function. I hope she can recognize this energy and release it. Let us wish her a life full of joy and happiness.

Please go through Adriana's Dui/Lake case (see pp.127–128) again by yourself. We discussed this case yesterday. The question was related to her grandmother's health. Now we can review another Dui/Lake case that is also related with health. This case is from my student Keivan's practice.

Student: Keivan

Number: 178

Corresponding Trigram: #2 Dui/Lake

Question: What is the situation of this new patient?

Analysis: The trigram Dui/Lake holds the postnatal position in the west, which is the prenatal position of Kan/Water. This tells us that Water is the root and Lake is the expression. The Water element contains the Kidney and Bladder organs, primarily the Kidney. Water is deep and often signifies a situation that is dangerous or will become dangerous. This could represent a serious health problem. Kidney expresses in the ears and controls the knees and lower back. Hearing may be a problem. Kidney energy is vitality, and a weakness in Kidney energy represents a weakness in vitality. Lake is the Yin Metal trigram that represents the Lung organ. Metal is important for circulation and communication. Because Water is weak, this patient will need to strengthen the Metal element, which is the mother of Water.

Outcome: A 51-year-old male presents with chronic hepatitis C. He is not too concerned because his liver enzymes have been normal for the last two years. He knows he should be taking better care of himself or this could be a real problem down the road. He has fatigue, especially from 3:00 to 5:00 p.m. He had to stop treatment with an acupuncturist in the past because he thought it was too expensive. He has a significant history of knee problems. His knees feel very brittle and are achy all the time. He had a bad car accident 35 years ago in which he broke both femurs and kneecaps. He was in traction for two months and in a full body cast for four more months. His left leg was set crooked and had to be broken again and reset. Steel rods were inserted into his leg bone. Ever since the surgeries, he has had tingling down his left leg, probably due to a nerve. Twenty-five years ago, he injured his knee playing tennis. Four years ago, he had another knee surgery to remove floating bodies. He also has a left shoulder injury that happened while swimming. He loves swimming but is unable to do it now because of the shoulder injury. His digestion is poor, and he cannot eat without developing lots of gas.

Wu's Commentary: *Keivan provides us with an interesting case through his insightful analysis. I will try not to repeat the information he brought to our attention. I have three reasons to say that Keivan resonates a perfect trigram for his patient: (1) The trigram Dui/Lake in the prenatal location is southeast and the related trigram is Xun/Wind. Xun represents the Liver and belongs to the Wood element and Dui is the Metal element. Metal controls Wood; therefore, it is no surprise that the patient has chronic hepatitis C. (2) 3:00–5:00 p.m. is the time of the Dui/Lake trigram time, so it makes sense to me that the patient has fatigue, especially from 3:00 to 5:00 p.m. Also, in the body, 3:00–5:00 p.m. is the active time of the Lung organ system and Kidney meridian system.[2] Because the patient has weakness in Lung and Kidney, he feels more fatigue during this time period. (3) Joints are related to the trigram Dui/Lake and the patient currently has knee and shoulder problems. Overall, the patient's health situation is a perfect fit with the trigram Dui/Lake.*

Here are my healing approaches: (1) Because the trigram Dui/Lake represents the Lung and breath, the patient should start practicing some simple breathing Qigong. It will help him strengthen his Lung function and reduce his fatigue. (2) Strengthen his Earth (digestion function) with the color yellow and display clay decorations in his environment. The patient has a long history of knee problems, which indicates he has weak Kidney function, even though the injury was from a car accident. This long-term Water problem (weak Kidney) would reverse control to weaken the Earth (digestion function). Earth element is the axis of the body, so we need to fix this axis first. (3) Use herbal medicine or acupuncture to fix the whole body system. I would recommend Shenqiwan 腎氣丸 if the patient likes to take Chinese medicine pills. I want to emphasize again that the way of Yijing is about change and should never be mechanical, especially when we use it as a guide for a patient. A corresponding trigram will help you to see a patient's situation clearly and it will help you find a correct healing approach, but you never use it as a doctrine for your healing process. Understand the case and find your way.

MOVE, TRAVEL, AND HIRE

I hope that I did not give you the wrong impression about my *Yijing* prediction system by discussing so many health cases. Of course, this prediction system works not only for health diagnosis and healing but also for any type of question.

---

2   Many Chinese medicine scholars and doctors don't understand the difference in active times between the organ system and meridian system. They often use the 12 meridians timing system instead of the organs timing system and thus misguide their students.

Actually, we worked with many different kinds of cases in my workshops. When I asked my students for permission to share their cases in this book, I got more responses from doctors and healers, most likely because they are accustomed to writing up case studies. Fortunately, my student Ryan sent me some cases that are not just about his clients. Some of his cases are related to his recent life experiences and I think these will be of interest to you. I add some boiling water to the moonlight tea, and then we can delve into his cases.

Ryan was planning to move to Ashland, Oregon, so he brought a question about it to our group during my Lifelong Training session in September 2007. The analysis was done by me during the workshop in these next two cases.

Student: Ryan

Number: 437

Corresponding Trigram: #5 Xun/Wind

Question: What can I expect from my move to Ashland, Oregon?

Analysis: The trigram Xun/Wind represents transformation, growth, music, and romance. Well, maybe you will get married there. As long as you keep playing music, you'll do great there. It might be a good idea to get a bamboo didjeridu.

Outcome: In three months, I got feedback from Ryan: "We have not yet moved to Ashland, Oregon. Kristin and I got engaged in Ireland and will likely get married after we move to Ashland."

Wu's Commentary: *In this case, we simply decoded the information from the trigram Xun/Wind itself. Remember, simple is the best way! Anyway, I hope to be invited to the wedding banquet so I can enjoy the Irish food and Guinness beer.*

Ryan also wanted to make a trip to Ireland with Kristin before their move, so he needed some financial support. He brought another question to the group during the same retreat. Here is the case:

Student: Ryan

Number: 323

Corresponding Trigram: #3 Li/Fire

Question: Will the financial investment I made five years ago pay off before I travel to Ireland in October?

Analysis: You will be financially supported for your trip to Ireland. The trip will be in the fall, and fall is the Metal element season. Your answer is Li/Fire, the Fire element. Which element is Fire's money? Metal, because Fire controls Metal. This indicates you will be able to get money for your trip.

Outcome: After three months, I got feedback from Ryan: "The actual deal I asked about has not yet paid out but I was supported for the trip to Ireland through another channel—a gift from family."

Wu's Commentary: We used the Liu Qin relationships to catch the financial support for Ryan's trip in this case. Please check your notes (see pp.137–138) if you cannot remember the Liu Qin relationships. The element to be controlled would be the money element. The Metal element represents the financial situation in this case because Fire controls Metal. So, anything that belongs to the Metal element could stand for the money in this case. Because the focus of the question is "need money for travel," we caught the travel time to compare it with the corresponding trigram Li/Fire. The time was the Metal season, which indicated they would have money for the trip. It seems that the actual "deal" he asked about would have been a large amount of money, so Fire would have to be strong enough to control the big, heavy Metal. My feeling is that he will be able to get it during the coming spring or summer because Fire will get stronger from the parent element Wood or brother element Fire.

Ryan owns a house in Portland, Oregon, that he wanted to sell so he could move to Ashland, Oregon. He wanted the house to be in a good shape before putting it on the market for sale. Therefore, right after the retreat, he needed to hire someone to repair the foundation in the northwest corner of the house. He narrowed down his research to three companies but he was not sure which one to choose, so he did three *Yijing* consultations to help him decide which company to hire:

Ryan's consultation A:

Student: Ryan

Number: 524

Corresponding Trigram: #4 Zhen/Thunder

Question: Should Company A repair our foundation?

Analysis: I meditated on the trigram Thunder and felt that for repair of a foundation, which requires stability, the "shifting feet" and shaking energy of Thunder was not a positive answer.

Outcome: I decided not to hire Company A.

Ryan's consultation B:

Student: Ryan

Number: 834

Corresponding Trigram: #2 Dui/Lake

Question: Should Company B repair our foundation?

Analysis: I meditated on the trigram Dui/Lake and felt the energies of marsh and moisture, which were the causes of the problem with the foundation in the first place. I felt that if I chose this contractor, the moisture problems would continue to undermine the foundation.

Outcome: I decided not to hire Company B.

Ryan's consultation C:

Student: Ryan

Number: 847

Corresponding Trigram: #7 Gen/Mountain

Question: Should Company C repair our foundation?

Analysis: While contemplating the trigram Gen, I realized that the prenatal direction of Gen is northwest, and the foundation problem was in the northwest corner of the house. I also realized that the trigram Gen represents honesty, trust, and stability. In meditation, we hold the back stable like a mountain to allow the Qi to flow freely. I received a strong message that this was the right contractor for the job even though he was $2000 more expensive than the others. He had a technique, which the others didn't, for holding the house stable while doing the repair work without having to raise or lower the level of the house.

Outcome: I hired Company C and am happy with the job they did. No problems.

Wu's Commentary: Ryan did a nice job of resonating the answer for his contractor during these three consultations. It is a great way to do different consultations for different objects or entities if you have multiple choices in your question. A clear question will help you resonate with a clear answer.

THE HOME OF YOUR SOUL

Jia (home)

In Chinese shamanic tradition, the physical body is the house of your soul and spirits. The healthy and peaceful soul and spirits will make the physical body their nice harmonious home. An injured soul or uneven spirit will have difficulty settling down in the house and may even destroy the house. Actually, the physical body situation is a reflection of the situation of your soul and spirit. I have found in my personal healing experience that many physical health issues are deeply rooted in the soul or spiritual level. This can be seen through their expression at the mental or emotional level because the mental or emotional expressions are the external appearance of the inner soul and spirit. You have to fix yourself at the spiritual level if your physical issues are intensely connected with your spiritual body. A trigram might help you find the connection. Let us take a look at some cases from my Lifelong Training session in July 2006:

Student: Tarana

Number: 675

Corresponding Trigram: #3 Li/Fire

Question: How is my client?

Analysis: The trigram Li/Fire indicates that your client is a middle-aged woman with a wide lower-body shape. She has eye problems and insomnia.

She has warming energy that wants to express her talent, but she has grief and sadness energy hidden within. This kind of energy might be related to her parents. Actually, the mental energy is the root of her health problem. The prenatal and postnatal locations of the trigram Li will help us understand this. In the postnatal arrangement, Li is south, which is the prenatal position of the trigram Qian/Heaven; and in the prenatal arrangement, Li is east, which is the postnatal position of the trigram Zhen/Thunder. Li belongs to the Fire element and Zhen belongs to the Wood element. Wood is the mother of Fire, so she got support from her mother when she was young. Qian belongs to the Metal element, and it represents father. Metal controls Wood, so this indicates that her father might have abused her mother. The corresponding trigram for the Fire element represents her. Fire controls Metal, which indicates she hates her father or, at least, doesn't like him.

Outcome: Tarana gave us some details about her client after the prediction: "The client is a 56-year-old woman. She has been diagnosed with glaucoma (increased pressure) in her left eye, and her vision has decreased. She sleeps poorly. She has a heavy lower body (pear shaped). She desires to express her creative energy but has great self-doubt. Her mother committed suicide when the client was 14 years old. She has a fantasy that her father killed her mother."

Wu's Commentary: The real situation shows us all Fire symptoms in this patient: pear-shaped body, vision decreased by glaucoma, and poor sleep. The best way to treat this patient is to apply the Metal element to bring down the Fire. It means she needs to work with her hidden grief and strengthen her descending Lung function. But the important healing approach for this client would be to cultivate forgiveness energy toward her father.

Here is another case from Tarana:

Student: Tarana

Number: 821

Corresponding Trigram: #5 Xun/Wind

Question: How about my friend's health situation?

Analysis: The trigram Xun indicates the person is a female in her early forties. She has a weak Liver function and finds it difficult to move. One of the symbolic meanings of Xun is Wind, and Wind represents spreading, loving, and sexual energy. Therefore, she likes to express her romantic loving energy but she has had anger and grief for most of her life. The root of her health problem is related to her weak Lung function. She has difficulty with her breathing. The prenatal Dui Metal tells us that this sadness energy came from long ago when she was a child or a teenager. She may have been violently attacked or abused during that time.

Outcome: Here is the feedback from Tarana after my analysis. "My friend is a 42-year-old woman who is bedridden with Multiple Sclerosis. She has severe Scoliosis and bad circulation. She has an aversion to many things such as going outside, the sight and fragrance of flowers, and germs.

She suffers physical, emotional, mental, and spiritual pain. She constantly feels victimized by a very harsh world and believes she is too sensitive to survive (although she takes great pride in her sensitivity). She is mystical, angry, depressed, self-righteous, and easily offended over imagined wrongs. She blames everybody around her for her condition and pushes people away when they don't do what she expects them to do. She writes tragic romantic poetry of unobtainable love. She is divorced but her ex-husband is like her slave. She still complains about his bad character and shortcomings.

She was sexually abused by male family members (father and uncle) and was abandoned by her mother as a child. She has not been able to heal this wound. She has mostly male friends. She has not done any of the suggested treatments and continues to deteriorate."

Wu's Commentary: A trigram gives information about the age and sex of a person, but don't apply it mechanically during your prediction, as I always say. In this case, I said, "The trigram Xun indicates the person is a female in her early forties." It would be a big mistake if I repeated this statement every time I got the trigram Xun in my prediction consultations. Each trigram carries so much information that you cannot rely only on intellectual analysis. Remember, the important part is to resonate with the trigram and the question through your heart. It is important to trust your flash of intuitive insight and not get tongue-tied by wondering whether it is right or wrong. Of course, this does not mean that you should always blurt out all of your immediate impressions. The important point is that as you develop awareness and deepen your understanding of the Dao, you will be able to sense the hidden meanings and resonances more clearly.

It would be difficult to reach a good healing result because her health problem is deeply rooted in her heart from the abuse when she was a child. She might not be able to realize this. First, we need to help her realize the root of her health problems, and then teach her some very simple breathing Qigong to strengthen her vital energy. The important part of the healing process would be for her to find real love and joyful energy in her life.

Motoe also provides a related mental health case:

Student: Motoe

Number: 975

Corresponding Trigram: #7 Gen/Mountain

Question: How about my friend's health situation?

Analysis: The trigram Gen indicates that this is a man who may be in his fifties. He has Qi stagnation. He may have back pain or digestive problems. The root of this problem is related to his Gallbladder Shaoyang system because the related prenatal trigram is Zhen. He might have suffered trauma in his earlier life because one of the symbolic meanings of Zhen is shock. This prenatal-related trigram Zhen indicates that he has frequent headaches.

Outcome: Motoe gave some details about her friend after my analysis. She said, "Yes, this is a man in his late fifties. His parents were divorced when he was in high school, and he has been angry with his father ever since. His father lives somewhere in California but he has not seen him since he left home after high school. He is a Vietnam veteran and has been very angry and sad about his experience in Vietnam. He was angry with his second wife, who divorced him. He often has headaches, back pain, and digestive problems (constipation). His biggest problem is thyroid, and he has been taking medicine for it."

Wu's Commentary: The real situation confirms that all his physical health symptoms originated from his angry mental energy. One thing that will help his health is for him to try to control his anger energy. One thing he can do is to get up early in the morning and go out into Nature and do some shouting. He should do this several times every day. Of course, for some people shouting only makes anger worse or reinforces bad habits. We have to look at the situation on a case-by-case basis. Often, counseling or psychotherapy is a good solution. But the most imperative healing modality for this person will be to cultivate his compassion energy and learn forgiveness. "Let it go" is a difficult thing for everyone to do; forgiveness is a derivation of "Let it go."

Let us review a case from the same retreat that is related to longing for love:

Student: Keivan

Number: 792

Corresponding Trigram: #0/8 Kun/Earth

Question: What is the situation of this patient?

Analysis: Kun is mother, Earth, Spleen, and belly. Earth element is the expression of what is going on for this patient. Therefore, this is an older female who has an Earth problem. Earth corresponds to the digestive organs, especially the Spleen. She may have a spleen problem. But this problem came from Liver weakness because it originated in the related prenatal trigram Xun/Wind. This trigram represents injury to the Liver. The emotions of hate and anger have caused the injury to the Liver. Problems are connected to her love life because Xun/Wind stands for loving Qi. Xun is Wood element and Kun is Earth. Wood controls Earth, so Wood is the husband of Earth. Therefore, she has anger energy within and this energy is related to her husband. She might have had the energy of hatred toward her husband in the past.

Outcome: The patient is a 55-year-old woman with liver cirrhosis due to chronic hepatitis C. She contracted hepatitis C through a blood transfusion during the birth of her daughter. She also has splenomegaly (enlarged spleen) due to the liver cirrhosis and portal hypertension. She is on the liver transplant list waiting for a "new" liver. She suffers from immense fatigue. Before Chinese herbal treatment, she had terrible digestive problems and severe diarrhea. She had a very difficult relationship with her husband, who died a few years ago of lung cancer. She started a new relationship after her husband's death and was much happier. Then her father died, and her relationship broke up at the same time. She has deteriorated in the last three months due to emotional upset and not taking care of herself.

Wu's Commentary: The healing approach for her should be one that nourishes the Liver, so releasing anger is very important. Chinese herbs can be used to nourish the Liver. Liver breathing Qigong will be very helpful if she could practice it every day. She should sleep with her head towards the east. The best thing for her health would be to find the loving relationship that she has been longing for.

Here is another interesting case from the same retreat:

Student: Keivan

Number: 121

Corresponding Trigram: #1 Qian/Heaven

Question: What is the situation of this patient?

Analysis: Qian/Heaven holds the Metal energy and represents a problem with circulation and Large Intestine. This patient might have a problem with the four limbs, but the center of this case is in the Stomach. The main reason is related to the prenatal trigram Gen. Gen represents the Stomach, stagnation, and blockage. It is possible that this patient has a long-term digestion problem. Consider the possibility of cancer, maybe in the uterus or ovaries. Energetically, this patient has too much holding. As a child, there were difficulties with her father. The root of the health problem is mental attachment issues. There is anxiety around her relationship with one of her parents, those who are supposed to take care of her. Anxiety is felt in the stomach. Her lymphatic system is stuck.

Fire is the mother of Earth. There may be a problem with Fire being weak and unable to generate enough Earth. The Fire trigram Li takes over the Metal trigram Qian position (south) in the postnatal arrangement. This refers to the circulation system and she needs Fire-Heart (love and joy) energy support because the Metal energy is too cold and is not circulating.

Outcome: The patient is a 54-year-old woman diagnosed with irritable bowel syndrome and fibromyalgia. When she first presented, she was unable to tolerate eating most foods without severe gas, bloating, and abdominal pain. Her body pain prevents her from being able to do much activity as her muscles and tendons are in a constant state of inflammation. She also suffers from terrible insomnia and awakens eight or nine times every night.

In a discussion about her early life, it was revealed that she had a very traumatic home life. Her parents fought frequently and violently. They were divorced when she was 10 years old. They both remarried when she was 12. The patient lived with her mother, and her relationship with her step-father was bad. She continued to be subjected to violence and verbal abuse, but it was worse. Her parents wouldn't talk to each other but used her as an intermediary through which to fight. She often needed to take care of and parent her mother. She was able to leave that situation when she was 17. She describes herself in those years as "just surviving" and that "what doesn't kill you makes you stronger."

Wu's Commentary: Mental stagnation will cause physical stagnation. In this case, the physical issues of this patient are the essential expressions of her disharmonious childhood that is deeply planted in her soul. In Chinese shamanism, the mind is the spirit of your Earth organs (spleen, stomach, and pancreas). If you have been holding something too long in your mind, it will express itself in the Metal organs (lungs and large intestine) because Earth gives birth to Metal. Lung is the ruler of your body rhythm, which includes your breath, joints, and tendons, so the patient has body pains. On the energetic level, the function of Metal is descending, and it can bring the Heart-Fire down to the Kidney Water to improve the whole body circulation. When Metal cannot function well, Fire will stay high so this patient has insomnia. As a healing approach, I would suggest this patient cultivate compassion energy for herself and send harmonious Qi to herself, her parents, and all the children in her life.

Before we finish today's discussion, let us look at a case from my student Ryan:

Student: Ryan

Number: 432

Corresponding Trigram: #0 Kun/Earth

Question: What is the core issue I am helping Jane with in this healing session?

Analysis: Doing this reading before the session, I knew that Jane's main issue was related to the Earth trigram. I felt that one of the main purposes for our healing session was to help her connect with her Dantian, her "home within the body," and to experience the world from this connection.

Outcome: During the session, she told me that she was having many issues around not feeling "at home" anywhere and she had an upcoming trip to Central America that was making her nervous. During the session, we focused strongly on her Dantian, opening the space within and feeling the sound healing emanate from her own "home within the body." After the session, she said she felt that she recognized her Dantian as a place she could enter and live within.

We also talked about how being connected with her Dantian would help her feel "at home" on her trip and would help her connect with her travel partner from a stable place without getting too caught up in the other person's drama (which was her main concern).

Wu's Commentary: To be able to "survive" in the modern, speeding life current, we have to put our attention on the schedule, appointments, bills, income, taxes, education, new agendas, endless paperwork, etc. Sometimes, we don't even have time to pay attention to our families. Of course, we forget the body and might never pay attention to it. And then this situation will cause the soul and spirit to separate from the body, and we will get sick mentally and physically, and this sickness can affect our families. From the view of Chinese shamanism, a harmonious and peaceful person is the foundation of a harmonious and peaceful family, and a harmonious and peaceful family is the foundation of a harmonious and peaceful community or society.

This case indicates that the Dantian is the home of your soul and spirit. Remember to take a deep breath into your Dantian, which will help you find peace even when you are having a difficult time. It will help you find your inner peace and harmony if you can take at least half an hour for yourself to pay attention to your body and Dantian and do some Qigong practice.

TAIJI QIGONG KAN 坎 (WATER)

It is almost 1:00 a.m. The moon is right above your head when you stand on the snow-covered ground. I take a deep breath with my body and the cold energy and moonlight give me the feeling of purity, clarity, distance, tranquillity, and the mystical. And then I feel my body melting into transparent, cooling moonlight. After about five minutes of deep breathing into my Dantian, I feel the cooling moonlight becoming like a warm spring in the body. We start reviewing the practice of Taiji Qigong Qian, Dui, Li, Zhen, and Xun. Then we hold the posture of the last movement of Xun for a couple of minutes and then start our new practice.

Movement: Start from the last posture of the Xun practice. Shift your weight to your left leg and bring your right foot close to your left foot. In the meantime, drop down both hands at the center of your front body with the left hand touching the Yin side of your right forearm (Figure 17). Then turn your right hand with palm facing down and take a step to your right side, shifting your weight to your right leg at the same time (Figure 18). Hold your right foot steady and take a big step to your left. In the meantime, draw an arch with your left hand to your left side and make a hook with your right hand. Keep your weight in the center (Figure 19).

Visualization: Imagine your whole body moving like a flowing stream. Your fingers are playing with a wave as you move your hands.

Function: Kidney is the root of your essential life energy and Water is the symbol for the wisdom. Your true spirit is rooted in the Kidney Water. You will easily be able to understand the *Yijing* knowledge and be good at the *Yijing* prediction if you have good Kidney function. This movement will help you strengthen your Kidney function and enrich your spirit and wisdom.

It is late. I hope you have a good rest tonight. It will be a nice day tomorrow, and I hope you will take it easy and enjoy Nature. Let us meet at 3:00 a.m. tomorrow and do something different.

Figure 17

Figure 18

Figure 19

GEN 艮—
DAY 7

Gen (mountain)

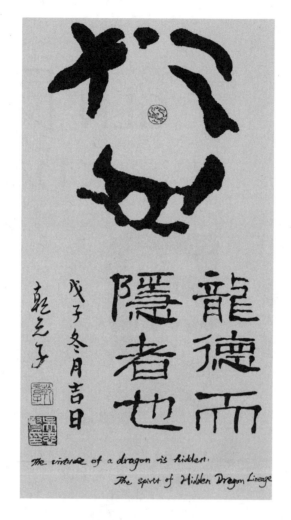

Long de er yin zhe ye

龍德而隱者也

The virtue of a dragon is hidden.[1]

---

1   See *Wenyan,* one of the *Ten Wings* of *Yijing,* for a commentary on the hexagrams Qian and Kun. See *Zhouyi Shangshixue* (Beijing: Zhonghua Shuju, 1988: 23).

7. Chuan 傳

The Hidden Immortal Lineage

Chuan (lineage)

In the ancient Chinese prediction teaching traditions, a person should first learn how to do inner cultivation before getting deeply involved in a prediction system. All prediction techniques are related to Shu 術, which literally means method, art, skill, or technology. In general, trying to learn something about Shu without doing inner cultivation will drain your Qi (vital energy) and Shen (spiritual energy). An expert predictor needs to do many calculations in the mind during the consultation that will consume the predictor's spiritual energy. In fact, it might take several years off a person's lifespan to pay the consequences of frequent consultations without doing the necessary inner cultivation. Therefore, in Chinese traditions, we always emphasize doing inner cultivation, which also includes the arts such as music, painting, and calligraphy.

All inner cultivation is related to the Dao 道, and Dao in Chinese means a path—a path to connect with the source of your life and the immortality of the universe. It will help you gain back your life energy and prolong your life if you practice a way of the Dao. According to Laozi 老子, we should Wei Dao Ri Sun 為道日損—practice with the Dao every day—and reduce. What should we reduce? Reduce excess thinking and action! Too much book study and intellectual thinking exhausts the Shen and causes the body to become sick. If you want to really practice with the Dao, then reduce unnecessary study and instead simply practice Wuwei 無爲, which means non-action or action-less. Wuwei implies tranquillity and naturalness, no action against the current of life.

The Dao is the ultimate source of the Shu. Inner cultivation will lead you close to the Dao and this is the true source of your prediction skills. The prediction methods and inner cultivation techniques we have discussed over the last few days were passed down by several generations of Laozi's students. I hope some of their stories will inspire your future cultivation.

A BRIEF INTRODUCTION TO THE CHINESE IMMORTAL CULTIVATION LINEAGE

I prepare Dahongpao 大紅袍 (Great Red Robe) tea for us. This tea is from the Wuyi 武夷 Mountain area in China. It is also called Wuyi Yancha 武夷喦茶 (Wuyi Rocky Tea). This is my favorite tea to drink before my Qigong practice or meditation. The tea leaves are large and long. They are from an old-growth tea tree. The color of the tea leaves is dark brown, which comes from its 50 percent fermentation process. This tea helps calm the mind and especially improves focus during the inner cultivation practice.

Wuyi Mountain

You might wonder why we are meeting so early today, at 3:00 a.m. The reason is that I want you to experience a very traditional way of doing the inner cultivation. The inner cultivation will really help you understand the *Yijing* and its prediction system. Whenever I spent time with my masters in their homes or temples, we would get up at 3:00 a.m. every morning, have a cup of tea, and then start the chanting, movement, and meditation practices. One of the chanting practices was to repeat the names of ancient shamans, immortals, and ancestral masters as a way to connect with their spiritual energy. Please take a look at this brief story about the ancestral masters before we start our chanting practice.

It is said that Xiwangmu 西王母 (Queen Mother of the West) was the first person to start teaching the Qi cultivation techniques to help others become immortals on Kunlun 崑崙 Mountain. In the Daoist tradition, she is addressed as Jinguang Xuanmu 金光玄母 (Golden Light Mystical Mother). The next important person is Xuanyuan 軒轅, the Yellow Emperor. He passed down some secret cultivation techniques of immortality after he became immortal. More than 2000 years after the Yellow Emperor, another very important person appeared in the Zhou dynasty (1027–256 BCE). This was Laozi 老子, whom we also call Taishang Laojun 太上老君 (The Most High Lord Lao). Many people benefited from Laozi's teachings, and there were two significant people among them: Shaoyang Zushi[2] 少陽祖師, whose original name was Wang Xuanfu 王玄甫, and Wenshi Zhenren 文始真人, whose original name was Yin Xi 尹喜. These two people started two immortal cultivation teaching lineages: Shaoyang Lineage and Wenshi Lineage.

Shaoyang Lineage is also called Quanzhen Pai 全真派, the Complete Reality Lineage. Shaoyang Zushi taught Zhengyang Zushi Zhong Liquan 正陽祖師鍾離權, one of the Eight Immortals of Daoism and Chinese folklore, in the Han dynasty (206 BCE–220 CE); Zhengyang Zushi taught two students: Chunyang Zushi Lu Dongbin 純陽祖師呂洞賓, one of the Eight Immortals of Daoism and Chinese folklore, in the Tang dynasty (618–907 CE) and Haichanzi Liu Cao 海蟾子劉操 in the Five dynasty (907–960 CE). Chunyang Zushi Lu Dongbin taught Chongyang Zushi Wang Yunzhong 重陽祖師王孕中 in the Song dynasty (960–1279 CE). Then Chongyang Zushi Wang Yunzhong founded the Northern Complete Reality School, and he had seven great students, six men and one woman: Ma Danyang 馬丹陽, Sun Buer 孫不二 (wife of Ma Danyang), Qiu Chuji 邱处機, Wang Chuyi 王处一, Liu Chuxuan 劉处玄, Tan Chuduan 譚处端, and Hao Datong 郝大通. We call them Beiqizhen 北七真, which means "Northern Seven Real Humans." These seven ZhenRen 真人 (Real Humans) all had their own schools and Qiu Chuji's Dragon Gate School became the largest and best-known school.

In contrast to the Northern Complete Reality School, Haichanzi founded the Southern Complete Reality School. He taught Zhang Boduan 張伯端, who was 83 years old when they first met. Zhang Boduan had spent many years seeking a teacher and he finally had a great opportunity to study internal alchemy. His Daoist name is Ziyang Zhenren 紫陽真人. He wrote the famous internal alchemy book *Wu Zhen Pian* 悟真篇 *(Understanding Reality)* and started the Southern Complete Reality School. He had five great students: Shi Xinglin 石杏林, Xue Zixian 薛子賢, Chen Niwan 陳泥丸, Bai Yuchan 白玉蟾, and Peng Helin 彭鶴林. We call them Nanwuzu 南五祖, which means "Southern Five Ancestors."

---

2   Zushi, which means "ancestral master," is a respectful title for those masters who have passed down their secret teachings, and Zhen Ren means "real person," a special title for an Enlightened Being who has successfully completed specific training regimens to become a "true man," "real human," or "perfected one" in Chinese Shamanic and Daoist traditions.

The Wenshi Lineage is also called Yin Xianpai 隱仙派, the Hidden Immortals Lineage, or Youlong Pai 猶龍派, the Just Like a Dragon Lineage, since the masters in this lineage were hermits, just like hidden dragons. Wenshi Zhenren taught *Yijing* prediction techniques and internal alchemy cultivation secrets to Mayi Daozhe Li He 麻衣道者李和. Mayi Daozhe passed his practice on to Xiyi Xiansheng Chen Tuan 希夷先生陳摶; also, Haichanzi Liu Cao, from the Complete Reality Lineage, passed his internal alchemy practices on to Chen Tuan 陳摶. Then Chen Tuan passed his cultivation and prediction secrets on to several students and two of them are related to our course: Huolong Zhenren 火龍真人 and Zhong Fang 种放.

Huolong Zhenren was hidden too deep and no one knew his real name. He did not teach his secrets to anyone until he met Zhang Sanfeng Zushi 張三丰祖師, who had been praying intensely for a teacher for over 30 years. Then Huolong Zhenren finally passed his secrets on to 67-year-old Zhang Sanfeng Zushi. Zhang Sanfeng Zushi passed his secrets on to several different students and he passed the Taiji Quan 太極拳 on to Wang Zhongyue 王宗岳. My teacher Yang Yongji 楊永積 was the 12th generation student of Wang Zhongyue and the movements we have been practicing every day come from his teachings.

Zhong Fang passed his *Yijing* knowledge on to Mu Xiu 穆修 and Li Gai 李溉. Mu Xiu had two students, one of whom was the well-known Zhou Dunyi 周敦頤 (1017–1073 CE) who wrote the *Taiji TuShuo* 太極圖說 *(Taiji Diagram Essay)*; the other student was the hermit Li Zhicai 李之才. Li Zhicai had a very well-known *Yijing* scholar and predictor student, Shao Yong 邵雍 (1011–1077 CE). Shao Yong was the first person to publish the Prenatal Eight Trigrams Arrangement and to describe its function to the general public. Between the Han dynasty and his time—a period of over a thousand years—none of the *Yijing* scholars knew of the existence of the Prenatal Eight Trigrams Arrangement. Shao Yong wrote many books about *Yijing*, such as *Huang Ji Jing Shu* 皇極經書 *(The Sovereign Limitation Classical Text)*, *Gu Zhouyi* 古周易 *(Ancient Book of Changes)*, and *Yu Qiao Wen Da* 漁樵問答 *(Dialogue between a Fisherman and a Woodcutter)*. Also, the famous *Yijing* prediction book *Meihua Yishu* 梅花易數 *(Plum Blossom Prediction)* is credited to his writing.

Li Gai passed down his *Yijing* knowledge to Xu Jian 許堅, Xu Jian passed it down to Fan Echang 范諤昌, and Fan Echang passed it down to Liu Mu 劉牧 (1011–1064 CE). Liu Mu wrote several books, including *Yi Shu Gou Yin Tu* 易數鈎隱圖 *(Yijing Numerological Secret Diagrams)*, *Xin Zhu Zhou Yi* 新注周易 *(New*

Commentary on Zhou Yi), and *Gua De Tong Lun* 卦德通論 *(General Discussion on the Function of a Gua)*.

These three people, Zhou Dunyi, Liu Mu, and Shao Yong, elevated the Song dynasty's *Yijing* research to a peak level in the history of *Yijng* through their great works.

THE CHANTING CEREMONY

Let us have another cup of the Dahongpao tea, and then we can begin our chanting ceremony. On the east side of the tea house, we have a small altar. On the altar are several small wood tablets with names inscribed on them. I make a big bow to the altar and then light incense and make an offering with a cup of pure water in front of the altar.

Then we face the altar and make three bows. First, we bow to Heaven; second, we bow to Earth; and third, we bow to all the ancestral masters and Enlightened Beings.

Please sit down and face the altar. Take a deep breath and adjust your breathing to be slow, smooth, deep, and even. Take your eyesight within and feel that you can see yourself with your inner eyes. Now adjust your posture: straighten your back so it is solid like a mountain. Lift your perineum to seal the Earthly Door. The Chinese name for Earthly Door is Dihu 地戶 and it is in the same location as the acupuncture point CV1. Pull your lower abdomen in. Open your chest. Straighten your neck and keep your head upright. Imagine your head touching Heaven with the Heavenly Gate open. The Chinese name for Heavenly Gate is Tianmen 天門, and it is in the same location as the acupuncture point GV20 on top of the head. Put the tip of your tongue on the upper tooth ridge behind your teeth. Close your teeth and mouth. Keep your shoulders down, arms relaxed, and armpits open. Bring your hands together in front of your chest in prayer position. I will start the opening by chanting in Chinese. Close your eyes with eyelids relaxed. Listen within to visualize my voice coming from your lower belly and feel the resonance through your heart and body.

After I finish the opening chant, please open your eyes and look at this tablet with the name of Laozi and the first four generations of his students:

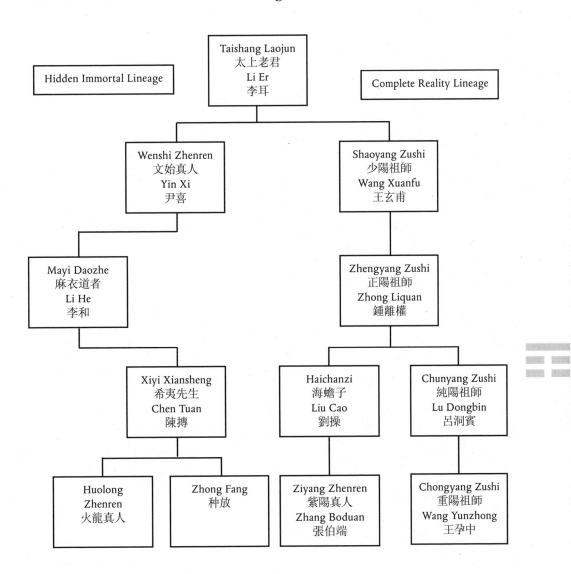

Let us chant their names three times.

Now look at this tablet with the names of the Beiqizhen, Northern Seven Real Humans, who are the seven students of Chongyang Zushi Wang Yunzhong:

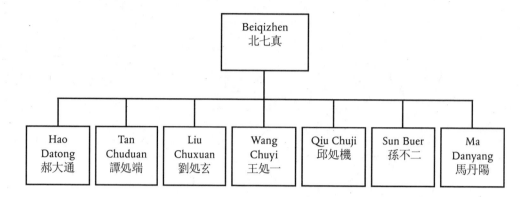

Let us chant their names one time.

Now look at this tablet with the names of the Nanwuzu, Southern Five Ancestors, who are the students of Zhang Boduan:

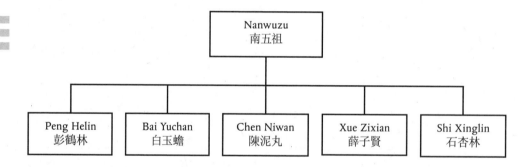

Let us chant their names one time.

Now look at this tablet with the names of the *Yijing* branch lineage masters:

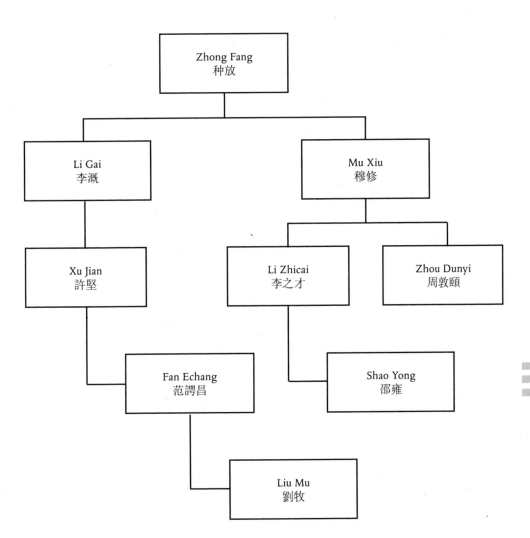

Let us chant their names one time.

Now look at this tablet with the names of the Taiji Quan branch lineage masters:

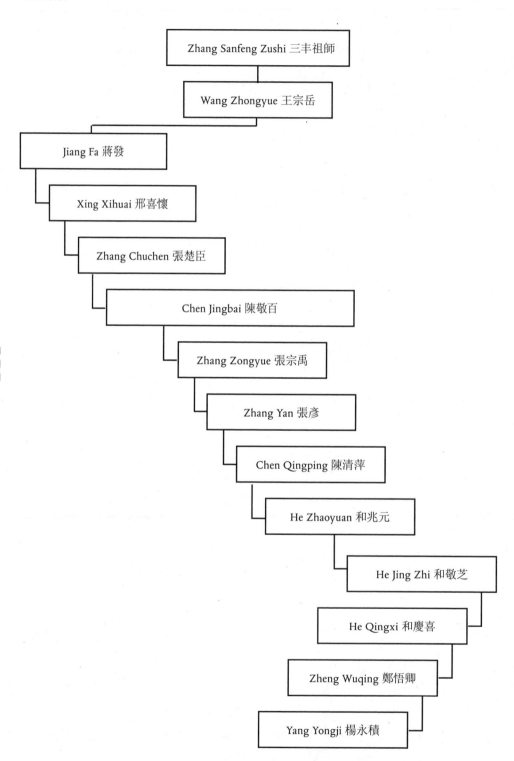

Let us chant their names one time.

Now bring your eyesight back to your Dantian and take ten minutes to meditate with this ancestral spiritual energy. Then I will start the closing chanting. Please listen within to visualize my voice coming from your lower belly and feel the resonance through your heart and body.

Please get up and bow to the altar three times. And now we can move back to our tea table.

MAYI DAOZHE 麻衣道者: THE DECLARER OF THE ORIGINAL *YIJING*

I make a new pot of tea for us. I take three sips of the Dahongpao tea, savor it, and feel more saliva in my mouth. I swallow the saliva down into my Dantian and then start sharing the story of Mayi Daozhe with you:

Mayi Daozhe was the first person to point out in his book *ZhengYi XinFa* 正易心瀍 *(Correct Yijing Heart Method)* that the original *Yijing* must have consisted of only the symbols of the Gua (trigrams and hexagrams). He emphasized that the written language text and the old commentaries within the *Yijing* book were more like footnotes to interpret the Gua than original text.

The original name of Mayi Daozhe was Li He 李和. He was very handsome and had beautiful hair when he was a little boy. He became a hermit when he was very young. He went to Zhongnan 終南 Mountain to do his inner cultivation, and then he met his future teacher Wenshi Zhenren, whose original name was Yin Xi 尹喜. The reason we have Laozi's *Daodejing* 道德經 to study is because of Wenshi Zhenren.

Yin Xi 尹喜 was a mayor of Hanguguan 函谷關 in Zhou dynasty (1027–256 BCE), and he was good at divination. One day, he felt a harmonious breeze coming from the east three times. Then he looked up at the sky and saw Ziqi 紫氣[3] (purple-colored mist) coming from the eastern sky, and he knew that an important person would pass through his area because of these omens. After a couple of days, he saw a man riding on a green ox coming from the east. He was shocked by this man's energy, and he knelt down at once and asked to be his student. Of course, this man was Laozi and he took Yin Xi as his student. Laozi

---

3 Ziqi 紫 is an auspicious omen in Chinese traditions.

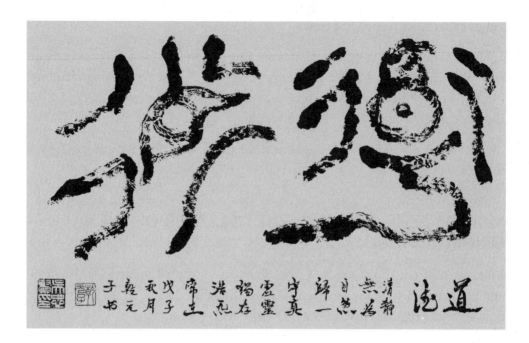

Dao De

Laozi

spent several months there and taught Yin Xi some Immortals' cultivation secrets and *Yijing* divination skills. When Laozi needed to continue his journey to the west to help others, Yin Xi implored Laozi to write something for his continued study. Then Laozi spent a few extra days there to write the *Daodejing* for Yin Xi. Later, Yin Xi became an immortal through his cultivation. He passed down his book, *Guanyinzi* 關尹子, which was titled with his name. We also call this book Wenshijing 文始經, which means the Classic of Wenshi. It is still titled by his name but it is his Daoist name, Wenshi.

After studying with Wenshi Zhenren, Li He resumed his hermit life. People occasionally met him and described him as having messy hair and noted that he always wore Mayi 麻衣, hemp clothes, which is the reason people called him Mayi Daozhe, which means Hemp Clothes Daoist Practitioner. He was very good at *Yijing* prediction and reading people's faces. Most of the time, he closed his eyes when he talked with people. He could tell what had happened in a person's past and what would happen in a person's future if he just opened his sharp eyes for less than a second. He passed down several books, and three of them are available in Chinese. In addition to the book I referred to earlier, *ZhengYi XinFa* 正易心瀍 (*Correct Yijing Heart Method*), one of these books is *HuoZhuLin* 火珠林 (*Fire Pearl Forest*), which is about *Yijing* divination techniques, and the other is *MaYi XiangFa* 麻衣相瀍 (*MaYi's Reading Face Methods*), which is about how to predict by reading a person's face.

Let us have another cup of tea while I share his student's story.

XIYI XIANSHENG 希夷先生: THE FIRST PROMOTER OF TAIJI

Many Taiji Quan practitioners thought that Zhang Sanfeng 張三丰 created Taiji Quan. However, this is not true. Taiji was in existence long before Zhang Sanfeng's teachings. Actually, the popular diagram of Taiji and the internal martial art Taiji Quan were first revealed to the general public through the teachings of Zhang Sanfeng's grandmaster, Xiyi Xiansheng Chen Tuan.

The birth story of Chen Tuan is interesting. It is said that one day during the Tang dynasty (618–907 CE), a fisherman caught a meatball wrapped in a purple cloth. He brought the meatball back home, made a fire, and was going to cook and eat it when, suddenly, there was a big thunder and lightning storm that shook the whole house. The fisherman was so scared that he threw the meatball on the ground. The meatball broke open and out came a little baby. The fisherman raised the baby and gave him the name Chen Tuan along with his own family name.

Chen Tuan was extremely smart when he was young. He enjoyed reading and could remember the contents of a whole book after he had read it once. He was also very good at poetry, and he wrote over 600 poems during his life. When he was young, he always wanted to be a high-ranking government official so that he could do great things to help people, but he failed the required exam each time he took it. In 931 CE, Chen Tuan was in his early sixties and he took the exam once more, but he failed it again. This failure totally broke his dream. Then he changed his mind and started his life as a hermit to do his inner cultivation. First, he spent 20 years on Wudang 武當 Mountain and learned the Zhelongfa 蟄龍瀍 (Hibernating Dragon Method), a special type of sleeping Qigong, from five old hermits living there. He often lay in one spot without moving for over one hundred days. Then he moved to Huashan 華山, Flower Mountain, where he met his two other teachers, Mayi Daozhe Li He and Haichanzi Liu Cao. He spent much time with Mayi Daozhe learning *Yijing* and immortal alchemy techniques. They often sat next to a fire stove, and then Mayi Daozhe used his iron stick as a pen and wrote his secrets in the ashes to teach Chen Tuan.

Flower Mountain

During his time in Huashan, Chen Tuan met Zhao Kuangyin 趙匡胤. This was before Zhao Kuangyin created his Song dynasty. At the time they met, Chen Tuan was very good at divination and he knew Zhao would lead his army to unite China and become the new emperor, so he passed his Taiji Quan on to Zhao as a way of supporting him. Zhao applied the Taiji Quan to his military training and was victorious in his efforts to unite China. Later, he started his Song dynasty and called himself Taizu 太祖, emperor. Because the soldiers had learned Taiji Quan from Zhao, they called Taiji Quan Taizu Quan 太祖拳 or Taizu Changquan 太祖長拳 after Zhao became the emperor. In fact, my master, Yang Yongji, had a very old version of the Taizu Quan book, and he told me that the form in the book was almost the same as the Taiji Quan form he learned from his teacher. Actually, one of the old names for Taiji Quan was Changquan 長拳, which means long form. The symbolic meaning is that you can continue practicing Taiji Quan without stopping, just like the Yangtze River never stops flowing. Therefore, Taizu Changquan can be interpreted as Taizu Style Taiji Quan.

After Zhao Kuangyin became the first emperor of the Song dynasty, he wanted his teacher Chen Tuan to come to his palace to help him. But at this point, Chen Tuan was over one hundred years old. He had been enjoying his immortal lifestyle for a long time and no longer had any political ambitions. After ignoring the emperor's invitations twice, he knew that he could not ignore the third invitation and would have to meet with Zhao Kuangyin. Before his departure to the capital, he went to say goodbye to his teacher Mayi Daozhe and humbly asked for his advice about how to free himself from the political burden. Following his teacher's suggestion, whenever he talked with the emperor, Chen Tuan pretended he had no idea about anything except his simple hermit life. Shortly thereafter, the emperor gave up and let him go back to Huashan.

In addition to the Taiji Quan, Chen Tuan passed down another internal martial art form called Bafa 八瀍 or Liuhe Bafa 六合八瀍. This form is becoming popular in the West.

Xiyi Xiansheng Chen Tuan wrote more than ten books on the *Yijing*, face reading, and immortal alchemy but only a few of them are still available in Chinese: *YinZhenJun HuanDanJue Zhu* 陰真君還丹訣注 is a commentary book about internal alchemy and *MaYi DaoZhe ZhengYi XinFaZhu* 麻衣道者正易心瀍注 is a commentary book on his master's *Yijing* book, *Correct Yijing Heart Method*. His famous book about *Yijing* symbolism and numerology, *YiLongTu* 易龍圖 *(Yijing Dragon Diagrams)*, has been lost, except for the preface. However, several generations of

Chen Tuan's hidden cave

his students managed to pass much of his secret knowledge of *Yijing* and internal alchemy techniques down to us.

Master Yang

YANG YONGJI 楊永積: A MODERN HERMIT

Yang Yongji 楊永積, also known as Yang Rongji 楊榮籍, was born in Rongcheng 榮成 County, Shandong 山東 Province in China. He was a Daoist master, Chinese medicine doctor, calligrapher, and martial artist. He grew up during one of the most chaotic periods in Chinese history: revolutions, wars, and natural disasters. He graduated from Huangpu 黃浦 Military School with a dream of world peace. During World War II, he was a captain and led his soldiers to fight for justice and peace. He felt deeply the suffering of the human beings during this time period and because of this, he left his military life and started practicing Chinese medicine to help others after the war. He saved countless people's lives during his more than 50 years of practicing Chinese medicine.

"You should know that a great hermit might live in a busy city" is an intriguing statement that the ancestral master of the Southern Complete Reality School, Ziyang Zhenren, Zhang Boduan announced in his internal alchemy book *WuZhenPian* 悟真篇 *(Understanding Reality)*. Master Yang Yongji was one of these city hermits and he lived in the city of Xi'an 西安.

Xi'an is an ancient city in the central area of China, and it is a great city for hermits. It takes less than an hour to get from Xi'an to the famous Chinese Immortal Lineage mountain of Zhongnan and its branch ridge Huashan, where the internal martial arts of Taiji Quan and Liuhe Bafa emerged. Master Yang lived there for over 50 years and spent much time in this mountain area doing his internal alchemy cultivation. Even in his old age, he still visited Huashan many times to connect with the spirit of his ancestral master Chen Tuan.

In the early 1950s, Master Yang spent time with many hermits and internal martial artists in Xi'an. Whenever I had a tea conversation with him, he was always delighted to tell stories about them. Sometimes, after he took a sip of tea, he would sigh and say, "You are too young to meet them, but it would be a great inspirational opportunity if you had just one chance to watch one of their incredible demonstrations." I would be happy to share some of their stories with you if you would like to have a cup of tea with me again in a few years.

Master Yang learned many inner cultivation techniques and martial arts forms from them. Besides the internal alchemy practice, he had three favorite internal martial arts forms: the Wudang Taiji 武當太極 form from the well-known Taiji master Zhen Wuqing 鄭悟卿; the Wudang Kunwu Jian 武當昆吾劍 Sword Immortal Form from the student of Song Weiyi 宋唯一; Zhang Xiangwu 張襄武; and the Tiandi Gun 天地棍 Stick Form from the Stick King, Wang Tianpeng 王天鵬.

Through these practices, he understood the connections among Chinese medicine, martial arts, *Yijing*, and internal alchemy. He discovered a special pulse diagnosis technique that he called Xuanmi Jiugong Maifa 玄祕九宮脈瀍 (Mystical Nine-Palace Pulse Diagnosis) through his cultivation. He could tell all the details of a patient's health situation with this diagnostic skill. In my memory, he always asked his patients not to talk when he worked with them. Then he would tell the patient what was wrong during his diagnosis and the patient would nod and say, "Yes! Yes! That's it."

Following the Hidden Immortal Lineage tradition, Master Yang was always very selective about taking on students. In general, if someone tried to study with him or asked him questions about martial arts, he would say, "I have no idea about that." But once he felt you were the right person to pass his knowledge on to, he would do his best to help you. In his entire life, he took only a few students. Here, I want to share a couple of stories about two of his young students: a Daoist priest, Feng Shiyao 馮世堯, and a Chinese medicine doctor, Xi Yong 席庸, both of them in their thirties.

Feng Shiyao escaped from his home and became a Daoist monk when he was 11 years old. Now he lives in White Cloud Temple in Beijing, and he is very good at prediction and Fengshui. I have met many *Yijing* experts, but I will say that their prediction levels do not reach Feng's by even 50 percent. Feng Shiyao is also an excellent Chinese medicine practitioner. Many times, I observed that he could tell what was going on with a patient just by hearing the name of the patient, even if he had never met the patient. He healed many patients who had been suffering for many years. I spent much time with him drinking tea and playing the *Yijing* prediction, internal alchemy, and Qin music together before I came to the USA in 2001. I knew that he had cured many different kinds of diseases that are considered incurable in Western medicine. Sometimes, he cured patients simply with his Fengshui skills. Of course, he is an expert internal alchemist and a great Qin musician.

Xi Yong started his Chinese medicine practice in Xi'an when he was 20 years old. You might not be able to find his clinic on your first visit because there is no sign to help you. Dr. Xi works in his clinic only two days a week so that he has time to do his writing and internal cultivation. You would see about 200 patients come to see him if you spent a day in his clinic. In general, he just talks to the patients about their health situations during his diagnosis, and then makes a formula for them. It usually takes him merely three to five minutes to finish with each patient, and that is the reason he can see so many in a day. Also, he is an expert Wudang Taiji Quan practitioner. He published a book called *Taiji Quan and Healing,* and Xi'an Television Station made a TV program about his Taiji form a couple of years ago.

Before my departure to the West, Master Yang told me, "The Great Dao exists everywhere without boundaries between nations; you should remember that and do your best to help others no matter where you are." About one month later, on August 18, 2001, Master Yang knew he had finished his mission in this lifetime. He sat up in lotus position at midnight and transferred his spirit back to his spiritual home, Huashan 華山. In 2004, after spending three years here in America, I had my first chance to return to China for a visit. During this trip, I felt so honored to represent the American Daoist Association and to help the Huashan Daoist Association and Xi'an Martial Arts Association organize the opening ceremony for Master Yang's monument in Huashan. If you have a chance to visit the Daoist sacred mountain of Huashan, don't forget to visit Master Yang's monument. After you pass through the main gate of

*Master Yang's monument
on Flower Mountain*

the Jade Spring Temple, the monument is on the left side in the temple. It should be easy to find.

I hope these stories will give you some inspiration in your cultivation. I take another sip of tea and then look off in the distance through the window. I see a golden-red cloud that looks like an eye that is opening in the dark clouds. Let us start our Taiji Qigong practice for today.

TAIJI QIGONG GEN 艮 (MOUNTAIN)

Suddenly, the sun jumps out of the clouds with his gentle face. I gaze toward the northeast and see the dark mountain covered with white mist, like an old Chinese Daoist immortal's landscape painting. I bring my eyesight back to my body and take a deep breath. Let us just stand quietly for a couple of minutes to feel the energy of this landscape through our breath. Now we can start reviewing the practice of the Taiji Qigong movements Qian, Dui, Li, Zhen, Xun, and Kan. Then we hold the posture of the last movement of Kan for a couple of minutes before we start our new practice.

Movement: Now start from the last posture, the Kan practice. Shift your weight to the left leg with your feet stable and toes grabbing the floor. In the meantime, change your right-hand hook position back to the open palm. Drop down your right hand and start drawing a big circle with the fingers of your right hand (Figure 20). Drop down your left hand and start drawing a big circle with your fingers. When you start raising your right hand, shift your weight back to your right leg. (Figure 21). Repeat, drawing these circles with your fingers 50 times. Then take a small step closer to the center with your left foot and at the same time, drop down your left hand with the palm next to your left leg (Figure 22). Take a small step with your right foot closer to your center and at the same time, drop down your right hand with the palm next to your right leg (Figure 23). Then stand stable with your feet shoulder-width apart. Take your eyesight within. Listen within. Breathe through your nose and your skin. Adjust your breathing to be slow, smooth, deep, and even. Feel each breath is related to your Dantian.

Visualization: Imagine your whole body is like a big mass of clouds moving, curling, and spinning when you are drawing the circles with your fingers.

Figure 20

Figure 21

Figure 22

Figure 23

Function: In Chinese shamanic traditions, cloud is a symbol for the mystical dragon. Wherever there is a cloud, there is a hidden dragon. And the dragon is an auspicious animal. It stands for transformation, communication, connection, and the universal way. Dragon is the rainmaker and has the magic power to bring nourishment to connect Heaven and Earth. Dragon can penetrate through rock or other matter without blockage.

The body of the human being is an energetic network. The body has its own energetic path of flowing Qi, just like clouds moving in the Nature, and your spirit is the hidden dragon in the Qi. Similar to the way moving clouds can make the rain and nourish the life energy in Nature, the Qi within your body has its own natural way to nourish your life and maintain the body in a state of health and harmony. Once the Qi becomes stagnant or blocked because of an incorrect way of living one's life or holding an incorrect attitude, the network cannot function well. This causes stagnation in the physical or mental layers. In modern times, this stagnation problem is described as different diseases.

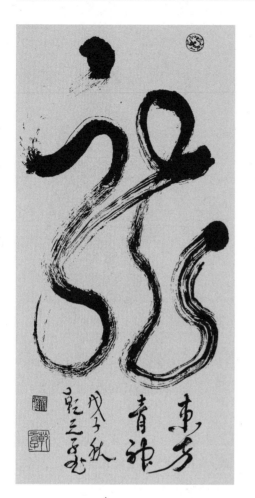

Dragon

This practice will help you transform your energy on different levels. In the physical layer, all the physical diseases are blockages of Qi or energy in the body. You can make your body Qi free-flowing to heal any physical blockages you have. On the spiritual layer, this practice can help you transform your spiritual body to a high level, which will transform you into a high-level *Yijing* predictor.

You can try to do the early morning chanting every day by yourself if you enjoyed our early morning chanting ceremony today. Tomorrow will be our last day to meet. Let us take it easy. I will see you at 1:00 p.m. tomorrow.

KUN 坤 ▬

DAY 8

Kun (earth)

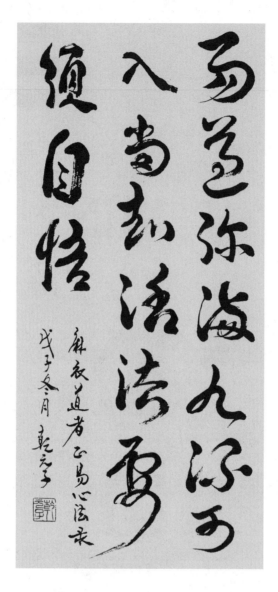

Yi dao mi man, jiu liu ke ru, dang zhi huo fa, yao xu zi wu.

易道彌滿, 九流可入, 當知活灑, 要須自悟.

The Way of Yi (Change) fulfills everything; you can use it in any kind of profession, but you should understand that Yi is vivid, and you must comprehend it through your heart.

Mayi Daozhe, *ZhengYi XinFa (Correct Yijing Heart Method)*[1]

---

1   Mayi Daozhe was a second-generation student of Laozi. *Correct Yijing Heart Method* is one of his rare prediction books that still exists.

8. Yao 要

The Essence of the Prediction

Change is the spirit of your *Yijing* prediction. To catch the true answer for your question from a Gua (trigram or hexagram), you have to understand the unlimited symbolic meanings of each Gua. If you want to be a good predictor, you must first be aware that the symbolic meanings of each Gua are living knowledge and not mechanical or dead knowledge, and then find a way to master this living knowledge. To start today's topic, I want to use a quote from the *Zhuang Zi* 莊子 (*Chuang Tzu*), "My life is limited and knowledge is unlimited; using the limited to pursue the unlimited is only exhausting to life."[2] This means that knowledge gained from external study doesn't address the root of True Knowledge and can only lead to exhaustion because we can never know it all! Internal cultivation leads to understanding the universal way through

Yao (essence)

---

2   Chapter 3 of *Zhuang Zi*. Zhuang Zi (369?–286? BCE) was a leading philosopher representing the Daoist strain in Chinese thought. The basic writings of Zhuang Zi have been savored by Chinese readers for more than 2000 years. Central to these writings is the belief that only by understanding the Dao and dwelling in its unity can man achieve true happiness and freedom, in both life and death. See *Chuang Tzu*, translated by Burton Watson (New York: Columbia University Press, 1996).

the body. The true and unlimited way to understand the outside is by cultivating and connecting with the inside.

XING 形: MODEL

I feel more relaxed today. After lunch, I take a slow "hundred steps"[3] walk to the tea house from my cabin. It is sunny and clear but freezing outside. The cold air gives me an extremely pure feeling as I take in the air with my body. It is a nice and warm feeling when I enter the tea house. I move the tea table close to the southwest side next to the window where the sunshine is coming in. Then I put a special brown clay pot on the little tea stove to boil water. I'm cooking a special kind of tea for us in this clay pot. Perhaps you have never heard of cooking tea, but some tea tastes better after it has been cooked.

I have the Puer 普洱 tea for us today. This tea is from Puer County, Yunnan Province in southwest China. It is about 80 percent fermented and it is easy to store and maintains its freshness for a long time. Fresh green teas maintain good quality only if you seal them well and keep them at a proper temperature; otherwise, the good Qi (energy) escapes from the tea. But Puer tea needs to be aged for fermentation and the longer the better (about eight years). The best way to make this tea is to cook it in a clay pot.

I tear off some tea from the brick of Puer tea, which is a dark brown color, and then put it into the boiling water in the clay pot. I continue to cook the tea on a gentle flame for three minutes. Then we move to the tea table with the pot of Puer tea. I pour the tea into two big cups in front of us. Please try it. I pick up my cup. This cup of tea looks like a cup of coffee because of its dark brown color. This tea is bitter and earthy without the aromas of other teas we had. But it is good for your digestion and will help to stabilize your Shen (spirit). Now we can start our last day's discussion with this tea.

In the past few days, we have discussed a model of the *Yijing* Eight Trigrams Prediction system:

- Meditate with a question and then spontaneously think about a three-digit number.

---

3   The "hundred steps" concept is from a Chinese saying, "You will live to be at least 99 years old if you take a walk of a hundred steps after each meal."

- Divide this number by 8 and use the remainder to find the corresponding trigram.

- Find the symbolic meanings of the trigram for the question.

- Figure out the trigram positions in the Prenatal Eight Trigrams Arrangement and the Postnatal Eight Trigrams Arrangement and the related trigrams.

- Categorize the Five Elements features of the trigram and decode the details using the Five Elements principle.

Although I emphasized that we should never decode a trigram in a mechanical way in the *Yijing* consultation, we should begin with the above mechanical model. After we practice it many times and really master it, then we will naturally be able to move to a skilled prediction level without following the mechanical model. This practice is similar to martial arts practice. The fighting skill of a high-level spiritual martial artist is formless. But you have to work very hard with certain forms for a long time to achieve this formless skill. A prediction model, which is a vehicle to access to the Dao or universal way, is like a form in martial arts. We might never be able to reach our destination—to be an excellent *Yijing* predictor—if we are not capable of playing with this vehicle.

In the beginning of our *Yijing* prediction practice, we need to learn how to analyze intellectually the corresponding trigram for the answer through the mechanical model. At this prediction level, we might make many mistakes and get many wrong answers in our prediction consultation because we have not mastered the prediction model adequately. We should allow ourselves to make mistakes but we should never ignore these mistakes. We should follow up each prediction case we do and compare the real outcome with the prediction to figure out which part was correct and which part was incorrect. This way we can discover the reason we got a correct answer or see where we went wrong. This is the right way to improve our prediction skills. *XuGua* 序卦 (*The order of hexagrams*), one of the *Ten Wings* of *Yijing*, indicates, "You will be a great predictor if you work through your mistakes."

WUXING 無形: PREDICTING WITHOUT A MODEL

After you practice prediction for a while, you might feel that the Yi 易 (prediction) is really Yi 易 (easy). Just like tea, after you have savored many kinds repeatedly, you will be able to discern the quality. You will gradually understand the

Wuxing

non-intellectual analyzing technique used in prediction. You would use the model-less way to do your *Yijing* consultations. You might be able to use different numbers or objects to make a trigram for your answer during your *Yijing* consultation.

The process for making a trigram with a non-three-digit number is the same as that for a three-digit number. Find the corresponding trigram in the Prenatal Eight Trigrams Arrangement by the remainder. In Chinese, we call this process Shu Qi Xiantian 數起先天, which means a number starts in the Prenatal Trigrams Arrangement and then we need to use the number to find the trigram in this arrangement. The process will be different if you use an object to make a corresponding trigram. An object is a postnatal existence, so you should use the Postnatal Eight Trigrams Arrangement to make a trigram. For instance, if someone comes from your east side to ask for your help, you can get the corresponding trigram Zhen/Thunder because Zhen is located in the east direction in the postnatal arrangement. In Chinese, we call this process Wu Cheng Houtian 物成後天, which means things are in the postnatal situation, and an object will help us find the corresponding trigram through the Postnatal Trigrams Arrangement.

When you apply the postnatal arrangement directions in your consultation, you should be aware of one important point. Don't try to find the direction by physical geography; the direction depends on you. When you do your *Yijing* consultation, you should assume you are in the center of the environment; you are facing south and your back is toward the north, your left is east, and right is west.

In the model-less prediction state, you can use anything as your prediction tool to decode the answer and never limit yourself to a mechanical model.

XINFA 心瀘: HEART METHOD

I take three sips of the Puer tea and feel the Earthly Qi moving down into my lower belly. Now, I'm going to share my prediction experiences with you through another case from my 2007 Inner Cultivation China Trip. I hope this story and my commentaries will give you some sense of the model-less prediction process.

It was the last week of our China Adventure, a time to relax, reflect, and integrate. We stayed at a posh hotel next to the Great Lake, just outside the beautiful Garden City of Suzhou. We were spending the time there to finish learning the Sword Immortal style of the sword form and continuing our study of the science of *Yijing* divination.

In the afternoon on July 20, 2007, it was typical summer weather in southern China. It was hot and humid. The strong heat wave made it difficult to breathe when we walked outdoors. Fortunately, we were gathering in a conference room with air-conditioning to continue our *Yijing* class. But the atmosphere was heavy in the room because Nic and Nora (who were on our trip) had just received a call from the U.S. telling them that their house in Portland, Oregon, had been robbed! It was a difficult moment for the group as most of us in the group are very close, almost like a family. To find out that our friends' house had been robbed was extremely upsetting, especially since we were so far away and couldn't do much to help. Since we were studying a *Yijing* divination technique, we decided to employ this technique to the robbery situation. Then we started the process:

"Can we use the address number of our house to make the trigram?" Nora asked. "Yes," Master Wu responded. "What is the number, please?" "5835," Nic answered quickly. We took 5835 and divided it by 8, which represents the Bagua. The result of this calculation is 729 with a remainder of 3. The remainder number 3 in the prenatal Bagua corresponds with the trigram ☲ Li/Fire.

Wu's Commentary: Here, we broke the pattern of the three-digit number model for making a trigram. On a model-less prediction level, any number, object, or quality, such as color, direction, shape, material, noise, or animal can be a model for making a corresponding trigram in your Yijing consultation.

Nic and Nora continue the story:

Master Wu pointed out that the image of the trigram Li is Yang outside and Yin inside (a Yin line within two Yang lines), symbolizing the weakness hidden inside the exterior armor. This can be interpreted as an untrustworthy person in the house. Also, Master Wu mentioned that one attribute of Li is that things might appear okay on the outside but that the inside is corrupt. Li is also a symbol for "middle daughter," so there was a suspicion that perhaps the house sitter was a woman who was involved in the break-in.

Wu's Commentary: Later, we had the result that the house sitter had befriended a man at a bar. She brought him back to Nic and Nora's house with her, and this man was the burglar. The lines pattern of a trigram holds countless symbolic meanings of the trigram; this is the key to open the mystical door of Fuxi's original Yijing. *You will never be able to master the spirit of* Yijing *prediction if you just confine your* Yijing *study to the* Yijing *written text. Please remember that the written text is only the commentary (or footnotes) to the pattern of a Gua (trigram or hexagram).[4]*

In the Prenatal Eight Trigrams Arrangement, Li occupies the position of the cardinal direction east. Moving from the prenatal arrangement to the post-natal and looking at the eastern position, we find the trigram Zhen, mean-ing Thunder. Thunder stands for shaking and broken. It symbolizes that the robbery might have been accomplished by breaking in from the east side of the house or it could indicate that the thief might live not far from the east side of the house.

In the postnatal Bagua, Li is in the south position, which is the position of the trigram ☰ Qian in the prenatal Bagua. Qian is Heaven, which cor-responds to the Metal element, the archetype of an older man or "father" and represents the person who needs to be enlisted for help to bring control to the situation. Master Wu interpreted this as a clear sign that there should be an older man, a father figure, or an authoritarian figure, like the police, who could potentially help control the situation and bring light to what had hap-pened. The Fire of Li needed to be contained by the cooling energy of Qian with its Metal quality.

---

4   See *MaYi DaoZhe ZhengYi XinFaZhu* 麻衣道者正易心瀍注, which is Chen Tuan 陳搏's commentary book on his master's book *Correct Yijing Heart Method*. This book was written in the 10th century.

Wu's Commentary: *In this part, we applied the "family member" information of the Eight Trigrams in the analysis: the "middle daughter" from Li and the "father" from Qian. Here are the details of the Eight Trigrams' family members: Qian/Heaven is father and Kun/Earth is mother. They have three sons and three daughters. Zhen/Thunder is the older son, Kan/Water is the middle son, and Gen/Mountain is the younger son; Xun/Wind is the older daughter, Li/Fire is the middle daughter, and Dui/Lake is the younger daughter.*

It was around this point during the divination that the air conditioner in the room stopped working properly and the room was getting hot. We were all fixated on the malfunctioning machinery, and it did not take too long before someone turned it to the correct setting and cool air filled the room again. Master Wu brought our attention to one vital point, that no external occurrences during a divination should be ignored because they could be a vehicle to access the Dao or universal way. This is truly the living aspect of the *Yijing* that is often not practiced. He emphasized that the burglary should be easily resolved because the problem of the hot air belongs to the Fire element and it is just like the trigram Li/Fire we got for the robbery situation. The cooling air belongs to the Metal element, and it is just like the trigram Qian/Heaven in the prenatal Bagua; therefore, the Qian (father figure) person would be able to cool down (fix) the heat (robbery problem) soon.

Wu's Commentary: *Waiying, the external responding factor, is always playing an important role in all Yijing prediction systems. It hints at the answer for your consultation. You should resonate to an external situation with your heart during your prediction. Nic and Nora's notes give us an interesting follow-up story:*

The first person who came to mind was our friend Arron whose nickname is AC, which is short for his full name. AC is a bit older and had a Qian-like position in this situation.

We took a break for dinner and debated whether we should call AC right away. We were hesitant to call at first because it was in the middle of the night in the U.S., but we felt compelled to do so anyway. When we called AC, he answered immediately and told us that he was with the police at that very moment. The burglar had been apprehended. When the police searched the burglar's backpack and apartment, the most valuable stolen items—a laptop computer, an old passport, and a social security card—were recovered.

When AC heard about our robbery, he investigated and found out from friends that the burglar was a well-known con man, always with the same mode of operating. That same night AC was out with a friend when his friend identified the burglar walking down the street. The burglar was trying to sell a bicycle and they approached him. AC's friend pretended to be interested in the bicycle while AC called the police. The police responded by searching his place and recovered some of our stolen property. I can only imagine the police's reaction to AC's investigative skills that helped apprehend the burglar within a day of the robbery.

Wu's Commentary: Nic and Nora had the perfect person to help with their situation because Arron's nickname AC is another Waiying (the external responding factor). AC is the abbreviation for air conditioner and the air conditioner cooled down the heat during our prediction. After we returned to Portland from the China trip, and knowing that insurance company belongs to the trigram Qian, I told Nora that she should contact their house insurance company because it might compensate their loss. I got the final outcome from Nora:

Our bad fortune did eventually transform into a comparable amount of good fortune. Our homeowner's insurance claim was approved, the thief pled guilty to felony burglary in the first degree, and the house sitter agreed to pay the deductible on the insurance claim.

To our surprise, the *Yijing* prediction was exactly on target. The people who helped to bring resolution to this situation were our friend AC, the police, the district attorney, and a judge, all of whom represented a Qian, Heavenly, authoritative, or fatherly position. Call my story what you will: randomness, coincidence, karma, fate, destiny, synchronicity, bad luck, or the *Yijing* in motion.

Wu's Commentary: Well, the universal way is always interesting. It seems that life is a game and the universal way is the list of rules of the game. If we want to be good at playing this game, we should learn the rules well.

GANTONG 感通: INHERENT PREDICTION

The symbolic meanings of each trigram are like countless fishes in the ocean; to decode the answer from a trigram is like catching a fish from the ocean. How can

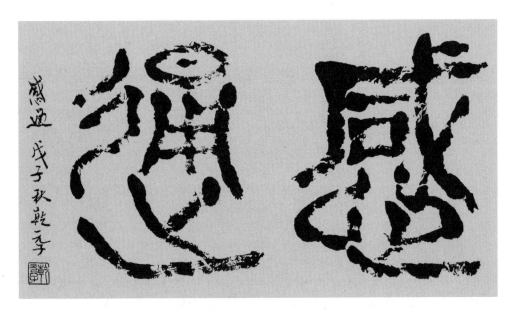

Gantong

you catch the specific fish you want? You might lose yourself and catch nothing if you jump into the ocean and try to catch your special fish. I'm sure you know the secret already. Just relax and meditate with your fishing pole, and the fish will bite your hook. Meditate with the corresponding trigram, and the answer will come out of your mouth through your heart. Since we will say goodbye today, I want to give you a little treat now. Please drink the Puer tea and relax for a few minutes.

I put my Qin 琴 musical instrument on my lap as I'm sitting in lotus position and start playing an ancient Chinese song for us. The Qin has a history of more than 5000 years, as indicated by a story about the ancient Chinese shaman/ king Fuxi. He invented the Bagua (the Eight Trigrams) and created the first Qin. Chinese hermits and scholars have been using the Qin as a vehicle for inner cultivation ever since. The Qin is a symbol for the universe. The size of the Qin is 3' 6.5" (in Chinese feet and inches), which symbolizes the 365 days of the year. It has seven strings to represent the Yin-Yang and the Five Elements (Water, Wood, Fire, Earth, and Metal). The top of the Qin is rounded and stands for Heaven; the bottom of the Qin is angular and stands for Earth. Therefore, the shape of the Qin represents the ancient Chinese cosmos, and the Qin music represents the rhythm of the Dao or universal energy.

It takes me about eight minutes to finish the piece. I put the Qin back onto the Qin table and sit next to the tea tray again. I pick up my teacup and savor the tea with the rhythm of the song resting in my heart.

Playing Qin

This was a great treat! The piece I just played is *Yu Qiao Wen Da* 漁樵問答, the *Dialogue between a Fisherman and a Woodcutter*. The fisherman and the woodcutter represent the natural way of life. The theme has been traced to an essay of the same title by famous *Yijing* scholar and predictor Master Shao Yong (1011–1077 CE). It represents the Daoist idea that one can gain great understanding by simply living in Nature without a formal education. I played this piece for you to emphasize that the secret of a high-level prediction is the result of inner cultivation. In my many personal experiences, the accurate answers will naturally come through my heart without any forced intellectual analysis when I am in a good meditative state during the *Yijing* consultation.

In *Yijing* prediction, we should understand the skill of Gan 感, which means resonate with the answer through your heart. The feeling of this skill is just as if we are playing the Qin music. When you play the Qin, your fingers need to be in harmony with the strings, then each of the strings needs to be in harmony with its sound (in tune), and the sound needs to be in harmony with your heart. With this skill of Gan, you will be able to reach the state of Tong 通, which means you know the answers completely in your *Yijing* prediction. *Xici* (*Appended Statements*) of *Yijing* gives us a deep insight into this:

> When you play divination, do no thinking, do no action, be silent, be still, and resonate your heart with the universe to clearly perceive the result of everything.[5]

We have many detailed *Yijing* prediction systems. The information I have shared with you in these eight days is less than 5 percent of what I understand about *Yijing* prediction. But the Gan and Tong that we have just discussed are the essence of all *Yijing* prediction systems. I want to pass two verses on to you for your practice from a Daoist poem, *Baiziming* 百字銘 (*One Hundred Syllabus*), the teachings of one of the immortals, Chunyang Zushi Lu Dong Bin:

> Sit and listen to the stringless music (Zuo ting wu xuan qu, 坐聽無絃曲).

> Clearly understand the universal secrets (Ming tong zao hua ji, 明通造化機).

What is the meaning of "stringless music" in the first verse? In Chinese wisdom traditions, we use the Qin musical instrument as a metaphor for the heart. We also call the heart Wuxuan Qin 無絃琴 (stringless Qin). Therefore, "stringless music"

---

5   See *Zhouyi Shangshixue* (Beijing: Zhonghua Shuju, 1988: 300).

Ting wu xuan qu (listen to the stringless music)

means the resonance of the heart. Let us try the Taiji Qigong practice one more time to experience this "stringless music" before your departure.

TAIJI QIGONG KUN 坤 (EARTH)

Walk outside to the southwest side of the tea house. It is a warm and sunny afternoon. I look down the hill and take a deep breath of the clear air. Cows are enjoying their pasture under the blue sky. Some of them are lying down and some are eating the grass with very gentle motions. I bring my eyesight back to my body and listen within to the "stringless music." After a few minutes of silence, we start reviewing the practice of Taiji Qigong Qian, Dui, Li, Zhen, Xun, Kan, and Gen. Then we hold the posture of the last movement of Gen with feet shoulder-width apart, and start our new practice.

Movement: Take a deep breath, then breathe out slowly and gently. Bend your knees while you turn your arms with palms facing forward. Shift your weight to your right foot and step your left foot backwards while you raise your hands

Figure 24

Figure 25

Figure 26

(Figure 24). Shift your weight to your left foot when your hands reach a little higher than your head, and then step your right foot backwards parallel to the left foot, keeping your knees slightly bent (Figure 25). Gradually straighten your legs while you drop your hands back to both sides of your body (Figure 26). Repeat this movement for a while, and then stand stable with your feet shoulder-width apart again. Regulate your breath from your lower Dantian. Soften your breath to be slow, smooth, deep, and even.

Visualization: Imagine your whole body melting into the Qi field. Feel the Qi like sunlight penetrating into your body through all the pores of your skin with each inhale. Feel the Qi condensing into your lower Dantian with each exhale.

Function: This movement maintains physical well being and awakens within us the eternal Dao, which is always present. The Dao is the ultimate source of the prediction skills. We need to move into the state of tranquillity to cultivate our inner knowledge after all active movements. Listening within to your "stringless music" is a way to experience the Dao. This is the essence of Taiji Qigong passed on by ancient Chinese shamans to help people learn the eternal Dao. Laozi explains this process in his *Daodejing* as, "The sages (shamans) conduct their business with action-less actions and give their teachings with wordless words."[6]

Thank you for your visit! I hope you had a great time here in my Celestial Tea House and have enjoyed this *Yijing* course. I hope to see you again on a new spiritual journey.

---

6   Laozi. *Daodejing.* Chapter 2.

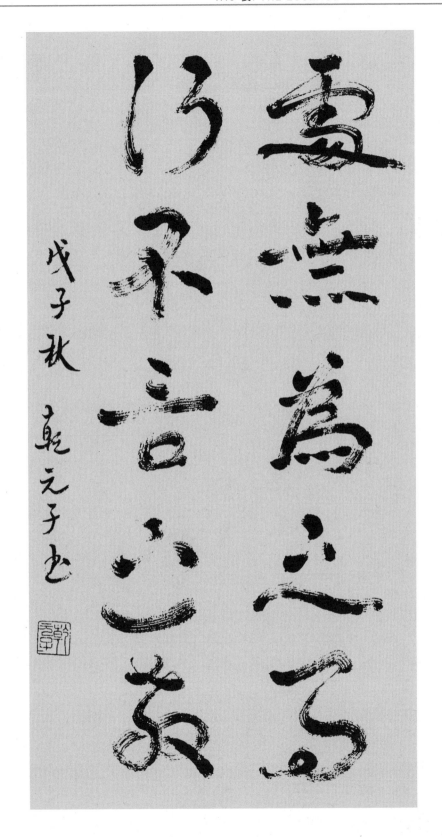

Afterword

Life is the Treasure

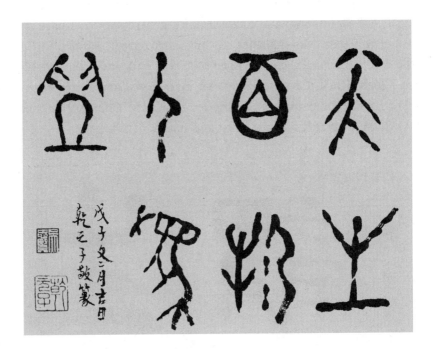

Tian sheng bai wu ren wei gui.

天生百物人爲貴

Heaven gives birth to the hundred things—among them, the human being is the most precious.

Bamboo Book from Guodian Tomb in the ancient State of Chu[1]

---

1   This Chu State *Bamboo Book* was discovered in the Chu State tomb (about 340–320 BCE) at Guodian, in Jingmen, Hubei, China in 1993, and was reprinted in 1998. See *Guodian Chumu Zhujian* (Beijing: Wenwu Chubanshe, 1998: 194).

There is a Chinese saying, "Tian shang yi tian, ren jian bai nian 天上一天, 人間百年." This means one day of Heaven is equal to 100 years of human being. The dimension of time is different between the spiritual world and the human being. You might be able to finish reading this book of my eight spiritual days within eight hours, but it took me more than 80 physical days to put together the information that I have studied over 8000 days.

Inspired by nature, I started this book in October 2006 during my visit to Salt Spring Island, Canada. After the first three chapters, I had to stop writing due to my busy teaching schedule. Then in November 2007, I made a decision to take some time off from my teaching so that I could have a personal writing retreat. Accepting David Branscomb and Laura Hauer's generous offer, I have spent two months here at Cloud Mountain for my personal retreat and writing. My Qin music, the sun, moon, stars, clouds, deep blue sky, rain, snow, hail, storms, trees, blue jays, Castle Rock, Cowlitz River, Mt. St Helens, and many other natural phenomena have accompanied me during my time here. The last five chapters are infused with the inspiration of the spirit and nature of this place.

"Generating and nourishing all living beings and it is called Yi"

Yijing prediction is magic, but it is also an art, a way of life, a way of nature, and it is a way of the universe. It is a way to express the great universal compassion, which gives birth to all beings and protects them. One of the definitions for Yi 易 from the *Xici* (*Appended Statements*) is "Sheng sheng zhi wei Yi 生生之謂易." I interpret this as "generating and nourishing all living beings and it is called Yi (changes or divination)." Good predictors should have great virtue in their lives. With this virtue, one will be able to cultivate the heart to perceive the answer to a question during the consultation and find a way to help others.

Life is magic. I believe that everyone has the experience of good time periods and bad time periods in their lives, but everyone is different. Some people may enjoy most of their lives, and some people may suffer most of their lives. There is always a reason hidden behind these phenomena, and in Chinese we call this reason Mingyun 命運, which means karma. The *Yijing* prediction or divination system is a way to help us to understand our Mingyun and guide our Mingyun to a better situation.

Yijing prediction involves much knowledge about how to help others fix their problems and make their lives or karma better. We did not talk too much about it in this book because this book just introduces you to the path of the original *Yijing*. As I have said, the *Yijing* knowledge in this book is less than 5 percent of what I understand. The knowledge of *Yijing* is vast, and you should find a good teacher to continue on this path if you want to be a good *Yijing* predictor or *Yijing* medicine healer. But I have always emphasized one essential point in this book: inner cultivation. Among all *Yijing* prediction knowledge, inner cultivation is the best way to help you learn *Yijing* and improve your life. Over my past 20 years of teaching, I have seen so many people cure themselves from physical and mental suffering and through their inner cultivation transform their lives into peace and harmony. While I was writing this, I received a story about a miracle from my student Cheryl Sly. She is willing to share her story with you, so I have appended it here. Maybe it will resonate with you and inspire you to continue your journey of inner cultivation.

Zhongxian Wu
White Snow Cabin, Cloud Mountain Retreat Center
Castle Rock, WA
January 29, 2008

White Snow Cabin

Appendix

A Miracle Story of Inner Cultivation

In 2004, I was flying from Portland, Oregon to Milwaukee, Wisconsin. It was an afternoon flight. I felt great and was excited about visiting friends and family there. Midway through the flight, I woke up to a number of people looking over me. I had had a seizure. I felt disoriented and definitely confused. Apparently, I ended up in the lap of a woman sitting behind me. The end of the flight finally came, and I was the last passenger allowed to leave the plane, as I needed to wait for paramedics to check me out.

I contemplated a lot that night, wondering what and why. At that point in my Naturopathic and Chinese medical student career, I had not had that much exposure to seizure disorders. I just thought the altitude or pressure must have done something weird to me that caused the seizure.

After two years and several doctors, I still had no answers. Fortunately, I did not have another seizure. However, I did have other symptoms that correlated with the seizure, but I did not realize this. For example, I had several hormonal symptoms related to my cycle and fertility.

In 2006, I was sitting in my endocrinology class and the professor projected on the screen in front of us the medical case history of a 32-year-old woman who had all the same symptoms I had, and she had experienced a seizure in her past. After testing, she was diagnosed with a pituitary tumor. These are usually benign but the concerns are hormonal irregularities and the tumor occupies space that can put pressure on the optic nerve, leading to long-term problems.

That day in August 2006, I made an appointment with a new doctor, one who had not heard my story. I requested a prescription for an MRI (magnetic resonance imaging scan) of my brain because I believed I had a pituitary tumor. The doctor agreed and, indeed, I did have a pituitary tumor in addition to a meningioma. Again, both were benign; however, they each have their complications.

The doctors insisted on either surgery or anti-cancer pharmaceuticals. I looked into both of these treatments and felt no need to take such aggressive routes. I hadn't tried every alternative and was then excited to help my body heal itself.

I met Master Wu approximately three years prior to this. Meeting Master Wu was a pivotal experience that forever changed the way I move through the world. Since meeting him, I have gone through times of intense dedication to Qigong and Taiji and other times when I didn't hold it as high a priority as the rest of the responsibilities I was caught up in. It was in those times of lack of discipline that I realized I needed Qigong and Taiji the most. Well, now came a time for some serious self-healing. Yet I was still unable to commit 100 percent to that focus. At that time in my life, I was struggling with several other obstacles that I needed to endure before I was able to focus.

In February of 2007, I reconnected with Master Wu for a weekend retreat. I left there inspired and walking strong again with the energy and the reminder of what I truly needed to do to become balanced again and to become ME again.

I began once again a strong, dedicated Taiji and Qigong practice every morning and evening, and during the day if possible. I remembered a story about a woman who was diagnosed with colon cancer that Master Wu shared with a group of us students he was mentoring. She had a professional artist draw a picture of a perfectly healthy cell. She put the drawing up on her wall and began a meditation practice focusing on that healthy cell. She did not do any other forms of treatment and after doing this for a length of time, she no longer had cancer. I decided to try that myself. Every meditation session/practice I would envision my pituitary tumor and meningioma involuting into itself and then dissolving into nothing. I did this every day and night for several months with no other treatment. I continued to have hormonal symptoms, but I continued my practice.

Then in June of 2007, I received a phone call from my sister-in-law who was upset and needed help. My brother and his family had been on vacation in California and were playing in a park when he had a seizure. They took him to the hospital to run tests. He had a brain tumor, only his was malignant, and he needed surgery within the next 48 hours. I jumped on a plane and flew to

California to take care of his children while he endured this process. He made it through and is now in chemotherapy.

After this, my family pushed me to get another MRI to determine my own health. I went to the Mayo Clinic because I heard that Mayo has some of the best doctors, and if I needed to do any other form of treatment, I wanted to discuss my options with them. The day I went back to the Mayo Clinic to find out the results of my MRI, I hoped to have time to swing by my apartment to pick up my past MRI results so we could compare the two. However, timing did not allow that, so I went there just to review my new results. There was no evidence of any tumor whatsoever. NONE! No pituitary tumor. No meningioma. Nothing! At that point, because this was a different doctor and establishment altogether, I felt that they looked at me as if I were lying, as if I had never had any tumor at all. They asked what I did to get rid of the tumors and I simply replied, "I meditated."

This experience has changed my life. I saw first hand the power of Qigong and Taiji and the universal energy force. I plan to share this practice with my future patients.

I am so thankful to Master Wu and his teachings.

Cheryl Sly, N.D, LAc.

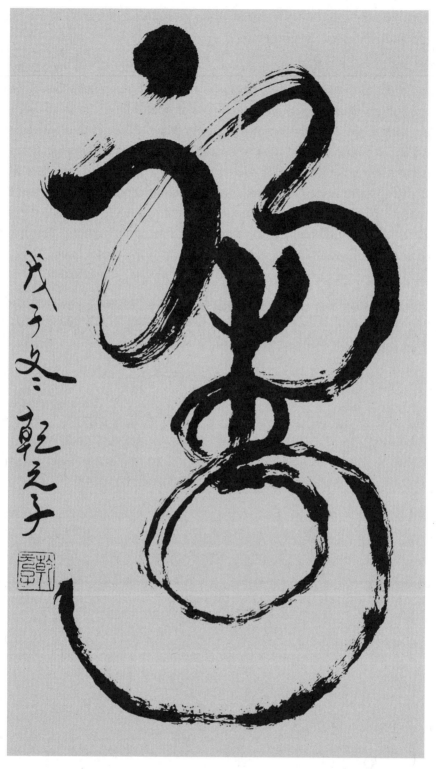

Happiness and longevity

About the Author

Master Zhongxian Wu was born on China's eastern shore in the city of Wenling in Zhejiang Province, where the sun's rays first touch the Chinese mainland. He began practicing Qigong and Taiji at an early age. Inspired by the immediate strengthening effects of this practice, Master Wu committed himself to the life-long pursuit of the ancient arts of internal cultivation. Over the next thirty years he devoted himself to the study of Qigong, martial arts, Chinese medicine, *Yijing* science, Chinese calligraphy, and ancient Chinese music, studying with some of the best teachers in these fields.

China's traditional arts and disciplines continue to be passed on within the time-honored discipleship system, wherein the acknowledged master of a given discipline instructs a close-knit circle of chosen students. Near the end of the master's life, the master selects the next "lineage holder" who will be responsible for the preservation of the entire system of knowledge. Master Wu is the lineage holder of four different schools of Qigong and martial arts:

- 18th generation lineage holder of the Mt. Wudang Dragon Gate style of Qigong (Wudang Longmen Pai)

- 8th generation lineage holder of the Mt. Emei Sage/Shaman style Qigong (Emei Zhengong)

- 7th generation lineage holder of the Dai Family Heart Method style of Xin Yi (Dai Shi Xinyi Quan)

- 12th generation lineage holder of the Wudang He style of Taijiquan.

In China, Master Wu served as Director of the Shaanxi Province Association for Somatic Science and the Shaanxi Association for the Research of Daoist Nourishing Life Practices. In this capacity, he conducted many investigations into the clinical efficacy of Qigong and authored numerous works on the philosophical and historical foundations of China's ancient life sciences.

In 2001, Master Wu left his job as an aerospace engineer in Xi'an, China, to teach in the United States. For four years he served as Senior Instructor and Resident Expert of Qigong and Taiji in the Classical Chinese Medicine Department at the National College of Naturopathic Medicine (NCNM) in Portland, Oregon. In addition to his work at NCNM, Master Wu was a sub-investigator in a 2003 Qigong research program sponsored by the National Institute of Health (NIH).

Since he began teaching in 1988, Master Wu has instructed thousands of Qigong students, both eastern and western. Master Wu is committed to bringing the authentic teachings of Chinese ancient wisdom tradition such as Qigong, Taiji, martial arts, calligraphy, Chinese astrology, and *Yijing* science to his students. He synthesizes wisdom and experience for beginning and advanced practitioners, as well as patients seeking healing, in his unique and professionally designed courses and workshops. Please visit www.masterwu.net for details about his teachings.

Master Wu has written six books and numerous articles on the philosophical and historical foundations of China's ancient life sciences, including the first Chinese Shamanic Qigong book in English, *Vital Breath of the Dao: Chinese Shamanic Tiger Qigong (Laohu Gong)*, also published by Singing Dragon.

Glossary

Bagua. The Eight Trigrams.

Baguan Yuce. Eight Trigrams Divination.

Baihu. White Tiger (in the west).

Baoxi. In most documents written as Fuxi.

Bazi Mingli. Chinese Astrology—or Principles of Your Karma.

Bianyi. Change. The second layer of meaning of Yi, representing the concept that the Dao expresses its way in different patterns in nature and in our daily lives.

Bu. Divination, or to divine. Before the Zhou dynasty (1027–256 BCE), there were two methods of divination: Rebu (hot-style divination) and Lengbu (cold-style divination).

Buyi. No change. The first layer of meaning of Yi, representing the concept that the Dao is always there and never changes its way.

Chadao. The Dao of tea, a way of classical Chinese spiritual cultivation.

Yinxianpai. The Hidden Immortal Lineage.

Dantian. Literally means "elixir field" and is located in the lower belly. Its function is to store the life force.

Dao. The universal way.

Dayu. Founder of the Xia dynasty (2100–1600 BCE), Shaman King who saw the significance of the Turtle Pattern and used it as a guiding principle.

Di. Earth (the bottom layer of the universe).

Dili. Earthly benefit; the right place for you to achieve your goal.

Dui Gua. Trigram representing Marsh or Lake. Carries the symbolic meanings or patterns of Metal, mouth, a beautiful teenage girl, joy, West, goat, shaman.

Fang. Directions, method, place, square, and way. The carpenter's square (see Gong). Fang is the way the ancient Wu applied the tool to understand the universe. It also represents the cosmos.

Five Elements. The universe is composed of the Five Elements (Water, Fire, Wood, Metal, and Earth) and everything can be explained in terms of these elements. They create a bridge of relationship between human beings and the universe.

Fumu. Father and mother element, in the Generating Cycle of Five Elements.

Fuxi. Sometimes written as Baoxi. Ancient Chinese Shaman King, inventor of the Yijing. In Chinese mythology the original ancestor of the human being through his marriage to Nuwa. He taught the first humans the necessary life skills, named the animals, and also invented many things including the fishing net, hunting, the law, the Qin (and other musical instruments), mathematics, Chinese characters, the calendar, and the city.

Gen Gua. Trigram representing Mountain.

Gong. Work, or to work. Originally taken from the Chinese radical (Fang) standing for the carpenter's square, then the universal measure, standing for order and correct behavior, or the law of nature.

Gongfu. Time, and also a skill that is developed over a long time and through strenuous effort. This implies rigorous repetition of drills, both verbal and physical. It also means "martial arts."

Gua. Hexagram or trigram. The trigram is formed from three lines: the top line represents the Heavenly way, the bottom line represents the Earthly way, the middle line represents the human way between Heaven and Earth.

Guangui. Officer and ghost. The controlling element in the Controlling Cycle of the Five Elements.

Guaxiang. The symbolic meanings of a Gua (trigram).

Guishu. See Luoshu.

Hetu. River Pattern. The basis from which Fuxi derived the Tiandi Shengcheng Shu.

Hongfan. Great Model. One of the oldest of the ancient Chinese classics, thought to have been written early in the Western Zhou dynasty (1027–771 BCE). Introduces the concept of the Five Elements and clarifies how the five numbers are related to the Five Elements.

Houtian Bagua. Postnatal Trigrams Arrangement.

Hua. Speak, talk, tell, speech, and story (see Shenhua).

Hulu. A gourd, but in Chinese mythology the vessel within which Fuxi and Nuwa floated over the great flood. In Daoist tradition, a symbol for the Dao.

Hundun. Chaos—the original eggshaped, dark chaos out of which ascending and descending Qi was formed.

I Ching. The Chinese name of *The Book of Change* written in the Wades-Giles system (commonly used before pinyin was developed).

Jianyi. Simple Change. The third layer of meaning of Yi, representing the concept that the Dao expresses its way in different patterns, and through vigilant observation we can learn by seeing the different patterns in the same object.

Jin. Forward, progress, and develop. The growthful phase of an element in the Five Elements.

Jing. Essence of the body, the earthly layer of the body. One of the three treasures of the body.

Jiugong Bagua (or Jiugong Bafeng). Pattern resulting from combining the Postnatal Eight Trigrams Arrangement with Luoshu.

Jiugong Shu. Nine Palaces Numbers, or the Magic Square.

Kan Gua. Trigram representing Water.

Kun Gua. Trigram representing Earth.

Lai Zhide. Author of *Zhouyi Jizhu*.

Laozi. Written as Lao Tzu in the Wades-Giles system. Great philosopher in ancient China and author of *Daodejing*. Also called Taishang Laojun (The Most High Lord Lao).

Lengbu. Style of divination relying on reading the pattern from the way horn halves fell on the ground.

Li. The philosophical layer of wisdom within the *Yijing*.

Li Gua. Trigram representing Fire.

Liangyi. Yin and Yang, the two components of life energy.

Liu Qin. Relationships—relatives and friendships.

Liuyao Yueche. Six Lines or Hexagram Divination.

Luoshu (also Guishu). The Magic Square. Original meaning "A Pattern from Lou River," from which Dayu derived Turtle Pattern, or Magic Square.

Mimi Mianmian. A way of breathing that is soft and unbroken, like cotton and silk.

Nuwa. In Chinese mythology, the consort of Fuxi and mother of the human race.

Pin. To savor or taste, but in its deeper meaning in classical Chinese culture it is the way of study and achievement of Enlightenment.

Pinming Lundao. Savor tea and discuss the Dao. A classical Chinese learning style.

Pinyin. Official Chinese system of romanization for the Chinese language.

Qi. Vital energy or life force, the human layer of the body. One of the three treasures of the body.

Qian Gua. Trigram representing Heaven.

Qicai. Wife and finance. The controlled element in the Controlling Cycle of the Five Elements.

Qin. Musical instrument dating back more than 5000 years. The first Qin was created by the ancient Chinese Shaman King Fuxi.

Qinlong. Green Dragon (in the east).

Rebu. Style of divination involving burning bones or shell and reading the pattern of cracks that appeared as a result.

Ren. Humanity/a person (the middle layer of the universe).

Renhe. The harmony of humanity; support from other people.

Shaoyang. Lesser Yang. Produces Kan (Water) and Xun (Wind).

Shaoyang Lineage. Quanzhen Pai, the Complete Reality Lineage, founded by Shaoyang Zushi. Later students founded the Northern Complete Reality School and the Southern Complete Reality School.

Shaoyang Zushi. Originally called Wang Xuanfu, founder of one of the immortal teaching lineages, Shaoyan Lineage.

Shaoyin. Lesser Yin. Produces Zhen (Thunder) and Li (Fire).

Shen. Spirit, the heavenly layer of the body. One of the three treasures of the body. Also means infinite, magic, marvellous, deity and divine, and to stretch.

Shenhua. Myths, the story about spirits or gods, Chinese mythology. Also, a doorway into the divine and an entryway into the mystery of the *Yijing*.

Shenming. Spiritual clarity, or spiritual brightness—the spiritual Enlightenment possessed by the Wu (ancient Chinese shamans).

Shi. Method of divination—a shaman who uses bamboo or yarrow sticks as tools for divination.

Shogua. One of the Ten Wings (commentaries on the *Yijing*).

Shu. Numerology, number or calculation. The numerological layer of wisdom within the *Yijing*.

Shushu. Deriving from Shu (number or calculation), the art of numbers or calculation, the name of the *Yijing* divination system in Chinese.

Shu Qi Xiantian. The process by which the trigram is found by using a number (rather than an object) in the Prenatal Trigrams Arrangement.

Shuiqi. Steam, vapor, or mist (water Qi).

Sifang. The four cardinal directions (north, south, east, and west).

Sixiang. Composed of Taiyin (Great Yin), Shaoyang (Lesser Yang), Shaoyin (Lesser Yin), and Taiyang (Great Yang). Represents the four spiritual animals in the sky: Qinglong (Green Dragon in the east); Baihu (White Tiger in the west); Zhuque (Red Bird in the South) Xuanwu (Black Warrior in the north). Also symbolic of time and refers to the four seasons of the year. The Sixiang produces by division the Eight Trigrams or Bagua.

Sun Simiao. Tang dynasty (617–907 CE) sage, revered as the "Medical King."

Taiji. Represents the universal life force.

Taiyang. Great Yang. Produces Dui (Lake) and Qian (Heaven).

Taiyin. Great Yin. Produces Kun (Earth) and Gen (Mountain).

Ten Wings. Commentaries on the *Yijing*, commonly thought to have been written by Confucius.

Three Treasures of the Body. Shen (spirit), Qi (vital energy), and Jing (essence).

Tian. Heaven (the top layer of the universe).

Tian Ren He Yi. The union of the human being and the universe.

Tian Shu. Heavenly book. Another name for the *Yijing*.

Tiandi Shengcheng Shu. Heaven and Earth Creating and Completing Numbers. Chinese numerological system.

Tianshi. Heavenly time; the right time to do something.

Tui. Backward, withdraw, decline. The declining stage of an element in the Five Elements.

Waiying. External responding or external resonance. A prediction technique.

Wenshi Lineage. Also called Yin Xianpai, the Hidden Immortal Lineage, and Youlong Pai, the Just Like a Dragon Lineage.

Wenshi Zhenren. Originally called Yin Xi. Founder of one of the immortal cultivation teaching lineages, Wenshi Lineage.

Wu. Ancient Chinese shamans. Enlightened beings. In addition to aiding others in transcending the physical plane, they governed ancient China and were also able to function as doctors and to avert natural disasters.

Wu Cheng Houtian. The process by which an object (rather than a number) will help to find the trigram in the Postnatal Trigrams Arrangement.

Wu Shu. Shaman's book. Another name for the *Yijing*.

Wuxing. Five Elements.

Wuxing. Predicting without a Model.

Xiang. Symbolism. Symbolic layer of wisdom within the *Yijing*.

Xiangqi. Fragrance (perfume Qi).

Xiantian Bagua. Prenatal Trigrams Arrangement.

Xici. One of the most important old *Yijing* commentaries. It literally means "Appended Statements." One of the Ten Wings.

Xiogdi. Brother and sister. The same element as the questioner in the Controlling and Generating Cycles of the Five Elements.

Xiwangmu. Queen Mother of the West. The founder of Qi cultivation techniques to help others become immortals. In the Daoist tradition, she is addressed as Jinguang Xuanmu (Golden Light Mystical Mother).

Xuanwu. Black Warrior (in the north).

Xuanyuan. The Yellow Emperor. Passed down secret cultivation techniques of immortality after he became immortal.

XuGua. The Order of Hexagrams. One of the Ten Wings commentaries on the *Yijing*.

Xun Gua. Trigram representing Wind.

Yao. The essence of the prediction.

Yi. The original meaning is divination or predict, but generally translated as "change" in English. The divination method embodies three layers of meaning of change: Buyi, No Change; Bianyi, Change; and Jianyi, Simple Change. Yi also means that the way of *Yijing* is simple and easy.

Yijing. The Chinese name of *The Book of Change* written in pinyin (official Chinese system of romanization for the Chinese language).

Yizhiyi. Properties of Change. One of the Ten Wings commentaries on the *Yijing*.

Yuzhou. The Chinese name for the universe. Yu means up, down, four directions (front, back, left, and right). Zhou means past, present, and future.

Zan. Ancient shamanic ritual with prayer or chanting.

Zhan. Divination.

Zhen Gua. Trigram representing Thunder.

Zhoubi Suanjing. Ancient Chinese text on astronomy and mathematics written during the Western Zhou dynasty (1027–771 BCE).

Zhuque. Red Bird (in the south).

Zisun. Children and grandchildren. The child element in the Generating Cycle of the Five Elements.

Index

Bold numbers indicate pictures

autumn, 38

back pain, 152
Bagua
   arrangements of, 67,
     68–70
   birth diagram, 91–2
   invention of, 66
Baguan Yuce
   divination case analyses
     see divination case
     analyses
   Five Elements, 86–9,
     131–40
   Jie Gua, 126–31, 196–206
   Magic Square, 78–86
   Qi Gua, 124–6
   Xiantian Bagua Shu,
     89–92
Baiziming, 205
Bamboo Book, 211
Beiqizhen, 174, 178
Bianyi (Change), 61, 62, **63**
Big Dipper, 20–2, **21**, 104
binary system, 66
Blofeld, John, 22, 36, 45
brain, 146
breathing techniques, 50
Bu, **48**, 48–9

Bushi, 50
Buyi (No Change), 61, 62, **63**

Celestial Tea House, 38–40
   features of, 103
   views from, 103, 106,
     107, 109, 110–11,
     112, 113–14, 115
Chadao, 38, 40–7, 60–4
chameleon, 20
chanting ceremony, 176–81
Chen Mengjia, 23
Chen Tuan, 183–6
chrysanthemum, 56
cloud, shapes of, **63**
Confucianism, 27
Confucius, 22, 27, 74
consciousness, 15
cosmic myth, 67–8
cosmology, 26–8
creation, 57
Cusheon Lake, **61**

Dahongpao, 172
dancing, 24–5
Dantian, 164–5
Dao, **36**
   daily life, 44
   inner cultivation, 172
   numerology, 77
   Yin/yang, 75

Daodejing, 183
Daoism, 27
Dayu, 81–2
Di (Earth), 26, 27
Dili, 17
divination, 30–1
   see also Bu; *Yinyang*
     divination systems

divination case analyses,
   about
   mental health, 158–65
   model-less way, 199–202
   move, travel and hire,
     154–8
   physical health, 146, 147–
     51, 152–4
   schooling, 151–2
Dragon Pearl tea, 41
Dui/Marsh, 69, 89, 90, 92
   divination cases, 147–54,
     157
   and Five Elements, 133,
     134
   symbolic meaning, 106–7

Earth, 57, 68

Fang, 25, 26, 27
Feng Shiyao, 188
Five Elements, 76, 86–9,
   131–40

Fumu, 137, 138
Fuxi (Baoxi), 25, 64, 65–6, 79–80, 203

Gantong, 202–6
Gen/Mountain, 69, 89, 90, 92
    divination cases, 157–8, 161–2
    and Five Elements, 133, 134, 135–6, 138
    symbolic meaning, 113–15
Gong, 25
Gongfu tea, 40–1
Gonggong, 68
Green Dragon tea, 41
Gua (trigram/hexagram), 40, 46–50, 58, 60, 76
Guangui, 137, 138
Guanyinzi, 183
Guaxiang, 101, 103–17
Gui, 47–8, **48**
Guishu, **82**, 84–6

Han San He Yi, 64
Hetu, 78–81
Hongfan, 89
The House of Flying Daggers, 147
Houtian Bagua (Postnatal Trigrams Arrangement), 31, **32**, 69–70, 128–31, 198, 200
Hua, 58
Huangdi Neijing (Classic of Medicine), 25
Huashan, **184**
Hulu (gourd), 65, **66**
human body, trinity of, 46, 58
Huainanzi, 26

Hundun, 57
Huolong Zhenren, 175

I Ching see Yijing (The Book of Change)
inner cultivation, 172, 173, 195–6
    chanting ceremony, 176–81
    heart method, 199–202
    inherent prediction, 202–6
    model, 196–9

Jianyi (Simple Change), 61, 62, **63**, 64
Jie Gua, 126–31, 196–206
Jin (forward), 139
Jin Tui, 139
Jing (classics), 20
Jing (essence), 26, 46
Jiugong Bagua, 83
Jiugong Shu, 78–86

Kan/Water, 69, 89, 90, 92
    and Five Elements, 133, 134
    symbolic meaning, 112–13
Ke (Controlling Cycle), 136–7
kidney, 146, 153, 154
Kun/Earth, 69, 89, 90,92
    divination cases, 162–3, 164–5
    and Five Elements, 133, 134, 137
    symbolic meaning, 115–17

Lai Zhide, 81, 87
Langer, Susanne, 100–1

Laozi, 174, 177, 181, **182**, 183
Leibniz, Gottfried Wilhelm, 66
Lengbu (cold-style divination), 49
Li/Fire, 69, 89, 90, 92
    divination cases, 155–6, 158–9
    and Five Elements, 133, 134
    symbolic meaning, 107–9
Li He, 181, 183, 184, 194
Li (philosophy), 29
Liu Qin, 137–8, 156, 201
Liu Wansu, 77
Longjing tea, 100
Lu Dong Bin, 205
lungs, 152, 154
Luo River, 81, 82
Luoshu, 81–3

Magic Square, 78–86
martial arts, 187
Mayi Daozhe, 181, 183, 184, 194
medicine, 27
Mimi Mianmian, 50
mirror, 151
moon, 20

names, 20
Nanwuzu, 174, 178
Nuwa, **65**, 67

observation, 100

Pin, 43–4
Pinming Lundao, 39
pork stew, 146
Puer, 196

pulse diagnosis technique, 187–8

purification, 41

Qi, 26, 38, 42, 46, 57

Qi Gua, 124–6

Qian/Heaven, 26, **35**, 69, 89, 90, 92

    divination cases, 163–4

    and Five Elements, 133, 134, 135

    formation of, 57, 68

    symbolic meaning, 103–5

Qicai, 137, 138

Qigong, 31, 38

Qin (musical instrument), **67**, 203, **204**, 205

Quanzhen Pai (the Complete Reality Lineage), 174

Queen Mother of the West, **76**, 173

Rebu (hot-style divination), 49

Red Phoenix tea, 75

Ren (Humanity), 26

Renhe, 18

San Zu Ding Li, 17

Shang Wu, 23

Shao Yong, 175–6

Shaoyang, 91, 92

Shaoyang Lineage, 174

Shaoyin, 91, 92

Shen (Spirit), 26, 46, 56

Sheng (Generating Cycle), 134–6

Sheng Ke, 134–7

Shenhua (myths), 56

Shenming, 24, 25

Shi, 49–50

Shu (numerology), 29, 76, 77, 124

Shui Huo, 133–4

Shuogua, 68

Shushu *see Yinyang* divination systems

Sifang, 25

Sima Qian, 22

Sixiang, 91–2

"stringless music", 205–6

sun, 20

Sun Simiao, 27

Taiji, 91

Taiji Hetu, 81

Taiji pattern in the Prenatal Trigrams Arrangement, **90**

Taiji Qigong

    Dui, 70, **71**

    Gen, 189–92

    Kan, 165–7

    Kun, 206–8

    Li, 93–5

    Qian, 50–1

    Xun, 140–1

    Zhen, 118–20

Taiji Quan, 180, 185

Taiyang, 91, 92

Taiyin, 91, 92

tea

    Celestial Tea House, 38–40

    ceremony, 38, 40–4

    and Dao, 44–7

    and Gua, 60

    types of, 75, 100, 124, 130, 147, 172, 196

    and Yi, 61–4

Ten Wings, 64, 170

thirteen, 83, 85–6

Three Treasures of the Body, 46, 58

Ti Yong, 139–40

Tian (Heaven) *see* Qian/ Heaven

Tian Ren He Yi, 24, **37**, 38

Tian shu *see Yijing* (*The Book of Change*)

Tiandi Shengcheng Shu, 80, 86–8

Tianshi, 17

trinity, 46–7, 57, 58, 64, 126

Tuan Yue, 21

Tui (backward), 139

turtles, 47–8, **48**

universe, 26

Waiying, 150, 201, 202

Wenshi Lineage, 175

Wenshi Zhenren, 181, 183

Wenshijing, 183

Wu (shamans)

    and Chinese culture, 25–8

    cultivation lineage, 173–6, 177–89

    meanings of, 22, 23–5

Wuxing *see* Five Elements

Wuyi Mountain, 172, **173**

Xi Yong, 188

Xi'an, 187

Xiang (symbolism), 29, 99, 100–3, 124

    of Bagua, 101, 103–7

Xiantian Bagua (Prenatal Trigrams Arrangement), 31, **32**, 68–9, 70, 128–31, 175, 200

    and numerology, 89–92

Xiantian Bagua Shu, 89–92

Xici, **54**, 64
  Bagua, 54
  dancing and drumming, 25
  divination, 122
  Gantong, 11, 205
  Hetu and Luoshu, 78–9
  numerology, 76, 90
  Tiandi Shengcheng Shu, 86
  Xiang, 98, 99
Xiongdi, 137, 138
Xiwangmu, **76**, 173
Xiyi Xiansheng, 183–6
Xuanyuan, 173
Xun/Wind, 69, 89, 90
  divination cases, 155, 159–61
  and Five Elements, 133, 134, 137
  symbolic meaning, 110–12

Yang line, 75
Yang numbers, 77, 80, 83, 87–8
Yang Yongji (Yang Rongji), 186–9
Yao (*Essentials*), 74
Yellow Emperor, 173
Yellow River, 79
Yi (ethnic group), 147
Yi (in *Yijing*), 20–2, 33, 61–4
Yijing (*The Book of Change*)
  about the title, 20–3
  premise of, 13–14
  spirit of, 30–3
  and spiritual cultivation, 42
  wisdom of, 28–30
Yin line, 75

Yin numbers, 77, 80, 83, 87–8
Yin Xi, 181, 183
Yin Xianpai (the Hidden Immortals Lineage), 175
Yinyang divination systems, 77–8
  see also Baguan Yuce
Yizhiyi, 88
Youlong Pai, 175
Yu Qiao Wen Da, 205
Yueguang tea, 147
Yunwu tea, 56
Yuzhou, 26

Zan, 74, 144
Zhan *see* divination
Zhang Sanfeng, 175, 180
Zhao Kuangyin, 185
Zhao Shuang, 77
Zhen/Thunder, 69, 89, 90, 92
  divination cases, 156–7
  and Five Elements, 133, 134, 138
  symbolic meaning, 109–10
Zhengyi Xinfa, 194
Zhong Fang, 175, 179
Zhongdao, 25
Zhoubi Suanjing, 77
Zhuyeqing tea, 124
Zisun, 137, 138